Stephen Castles has been Head of the Centre for Multicultural Studies at the University of Wollongong since early 1986. Previously he was involved in teaching, migration research and community work in West Germany, Britain and Africa. He is author of *Here for Good — Western Europe's New Ethnic Minorities* (Pluto Press, 1984), and co-author of *Immigrant Workers and Class Structure in Western Europe*, (Oxford University Press, 1973 and 1985), and *The Education of the Future* (Pluto Press, 1979).

Bill Cope has been a research fellow at the Centre for Multicultural Studies since 1984. His main areas of interest are multicultural education and historical research into the questions of Australian identity. On this latter theme, his Ph.D traced changes in Australian identity as reflected in history and social studies textbooks since 1945. He has published widely on multicultural education and curriculum theory, as well as being actively involved in the Social Literacy curriculum project since 1979.

Mary Kalantzis is a research fellow at the Centre for Multicultural Studies where she has worked since 1984. Her main publications include *The Language Question: The Maintenance of Languages other than English,* a two-volume report to the Department of Immigration and Ethnic Affairs; numerous commissioned research reports and academic articles in the area of multiculturalism and education and co-authorship of the extensive Social Literacy series of books for primary and secondary schools.

Michael Morrissey is Associate Head of the Centre for Multi-cultural Studies where he has worked since 1980. Previously he has taught at the Universities of Sierra Leone, Exeter, Glasgow and New South Wales. His main interest is in the role of ethnicity and race in the labour process, on which he has published extensively.

Stephen Castles
Bill Cope
Mary Kalantzis
Michael Morrissey

Mistaken Identity

Multiculturalism and
the Demise of
Nationalism in Australia

Pluto  Press
Sydney

First published in 1988 by Pluto Press Australia,
Limited,
PO Box 199, Leichhardt, NSW 2040

Typeset, printed and bound by Southwood Press,
80 Chapel Street, Marrickville, NSW 2204

Cover design by Donna Rawlins

Mistaken Identity: Multiculturalism and the
Demise of Nationalism in Australia
Bibliography

ISBN 0 949138 21 5
1. Pluralism (Social sciences) 2. Ethnicity —
Australia. 3. Nationalism — Australia. 4. Minorities
— Australia. 5. Australia — Ethnic relations.
I. Castles, Stephen.
306'.0994

Contents

Preface

This book was written jointly by four researchers at the Centre for Multicultural Studies at the University of Wollongong. The C.M.S. was set up in 1978 to carry out research and teaching on the impact of immigration on Australian society. We see this book as part of that task, but also as part of a wider debate on the future path which Australia can and should pursue.

The text is a result of discussions within the Centre, as well as with friends and colleagues outside. It is a collective work in the sense that we all discussed and worked on all aspects though first drafts were written by individuals. It is in the nature of the complexity and controversy of the theme, that we did not finally agree on all issues. The book is therefore part of a continuing debate, between ourselves and with others.

Some parts were presented as seminar papers at Wollongong University and we thank all participants for their ideas and criticism.

We also thank the following people, who read parts of the text and made suggestions: Caroline Alcorso, Paula Hamilton, and Wiebke Wüstenburg.

We thank Ric Sissons of Pluto Press for his patient support, and Stephanie Dowrick for her thorough editing.

Last, but not least, we express our gratitude to Carlene Robinson and Tina Kungl for processing so many words, so many times.

1.
A Nation Without Nationalism?

By international and historical standards, Australia is a very quiet *quiet* place. Despite this appearance, things of world-historical significance have happened here. Few conquests have been so systematic and brutal as that of Aboriginal society. Here our quiet is deceptively a product of the very severity of the conquest and, consequently, an active silencing of historical guilt and possible arguments about reparations. The other event of world-historical importance is Australia's post-war immigration. Again, the quiet of this place deceives. It has been a programme of incomparable size internationally in the past half-century: a First World society with low birth rates has doubled its population, to a significant extent through immigration, in forty years. No other country has accepted so many immigrants in this period relative to the size of the existing population, bar the peculiar historical phenomenon of the attempt to establish the state of Israel in Palestine. No other nation-state has been as actively involved in the recruitment of immigrants. Nowhere have the sources of immigrants been so diverse.

Yet Australia is still comparatively a quiet place, at least compared *homogen⁵* to Belfast or New York, Jerusalem or Liverpool. Looking ahead hypothetically from 1945 with knowledge of the immigration that would take place over the following four decades, one could hardly have predicted the quiet. Ninety per cent of the population then was Australian-born and English-speaking. The Irish-English divide had been settled, even if it had not been finally resolved. In terms of cultural identity and aspirations, Australia was an unusually homogeneous society. A central part of this homogeneity was a persistent culture of racism manifest most prominently in contempt for the Aborigines and fear of the 'yellow peril' to Australia's north. Racism against immigrants had become a virulent element of Australian identity in the nineteenth-century experience of relations with Chinese on the goldfields and 'coolie' and 'Kanaka' labour. This *racist* carried through in the White Australia Policy of the twentieth century, and racist ideology about Asia that came with fighting the Japanese in the Second World War.

Most remarkable, then, is that the quiet should have been maintained. Not only does the quiet and apparent lack of history mask some significant historical events, the quiet itself is a remarkable historical phenomenon. This book is about the demise of traditional forms of nationalism in Australia and the rise of multiculturalism. It is about the changes that have occurred in Australian society in the past forty years and the effects these have had on national or cultural identity.

To begin, we pose some of the most difficult questions about nation, culture, racism and identity through a collage of recent public statements.

Drawing boundaries

We are a people of many nations, each having our own tribal boundaries and each living with and adapting to different living conditions. Each tribe only hunted within their boundaries, controlled burning was used so new plant life grew and more animal life came. Food from the land was shared equally among the people. There is no waste, we never take more than we need, keeping the cycle of life producing from the land to us without destroying. Ceremonies of song and dance in respect of the land are done showing the appreciation of what it gives and provides. When the white man, who has no spiritual contact with the land, came, he knew only one way to treat the land — by raping and destroying. They only wanted the land for greed, totally ignoring our people's spiritual rights to the land, desecrating a culture and a people of nature. (*Land is Life,1988 Big Red Diary*)

NSW Aborigines who 'terrorized' the border town of Goondiwindi at the weekend should be jailed 'to set an example', a Queensland Cabinet minister said yesterday. The Minister for Industry and Technology, Mr Peter McKechie, said after visiting Goondiwindi that NSW Aborigines 'belted up people at random' in the riot, which resulted in $20,000 damage and injuries to 10 people. The Moree Aboriginal Legal Service accused the minister of racism and of trying to pre-empt police inquiries into the incident. (*Sydney Morning Herald*, 14 January 1987)

The faded idea of a national treaty, such as has occurred in Canada, New Zealand and other dominions of the Crown, should be revived. Some thoughtful commentators on the current Australian scene warn that unless national initiatives are taken, there may be a danger that Australia could follow South Africa as a pariah of the international community. The brave hope of enlivening the national conscience in time for action to coincide with the Bicentenary seems to be fading. But is it too late to use

that national celebration as an occasion for national reconcil-
iation upon terms which are practical and just and remove the
blight of two centuries of injustice and neglect? (Justice Michael
Kirby, President of the NSW Court of Appeal in the *Sydney
Morning Herald*, 6 March 1987)

People need to feel they belong to their country. Their need for *Blainey*
community is most pronounced at a time of adversity. The people
who are hit hardest by a depression, who feel their children will
suffer, look for loyalty from the rest of the community and the
government. The present immigration programme, in its indif-
ference to the feelings of old Australians, erodes those loyalties.
The multicultural policy, and its emphasis on what is different
and on the rights of the new minority rather than the old majority,
gnaws at that sense of solidarity that many people crave for. The
policy of governments since 1978 to turn Australia into a land of
all nations runs across the present yearning for stability and social
cohesion. (Geoffrey Blainey, *All for Australia*, 1984)

Acquiring Australian Citizenship should not require suppres-
sion of one's cultural heritage or identity. Rather, the act of
becoming a citizen is — symbolically and actually — a process of
bringing one's own gift of language, culture and traditions to
enrich the already diverse fabric of Australian society. Our vision
of a multicultural society shares with our concept of citizenship, a
strong emphasis on building a cohesive and harmonious society
which is all the more tolerant and outward-looking because of the
diversity of its origins. (Ministerial Statement, Mr Ian MacPhee,
Minister for Immigration and Ethnic Affairs, 6 May 1982)

Discrimination against women and immigrant workers remains
deeply entrenched at Australia Post despite its equal employment
opportunity policies, according to an internal Australia Post
study obtained by the *Herald*. The study found that women and
immigrants, Vietnamese in particular, are not being promoted
because of widespread prejudice within Australia Post, and that
many workers believed that discrimination was necessary for the
organization to function effectively. (*Sydney Morning Herald*, 5
May 1987)

If we do not do something we will continually see government
surrendering to special interest groups like the ESL. Its clients
routinely slaughter goat kids facing Mecca in living rooms in
suburban Lakemba. How was Gallipoli looking down to Suvla
Bay? (Des Keegan, *The Australian*, 9 September 1986)

Multiculturalism will have real meaning in Australia when the
English are seen as one group of ethnics among others and when
Queen Elizabeth will be welcomed as a representative of one of
Australia's honoured ethnic communities. Just as whites can be
seen as the black problem, or men as the woman problem, so, in a

multicultural sense, those Australians who still define Australia by its Britishness might be seen as the ethnic problem: they are, in effect, the principal enemies of policies of cultural diversity. (Donald Horne, *The Perils of Multiculturalism as a National Ideal*, 1983)

Lebanese and Vietnamese voters are shifting their support from Labor to the Liberal Party in large numbers and could play a decisive role in any electoral reversal for the State Government in the forthcoming by-elections . . . Dr Forest said the study showed the ethnic vote was significant and that 'politicians can benefit from wooing migrant workers in the forthcoming elections'. (*Sydney Morning Herald*, 23 January 1987)

Defining Australia

According to Benedict Anderson, 1987 was the 200th anniversary of the birth of the nation state. The 'extraordinary invention' which was to become an 'unproblematic planetary norm' came to the world, says Anderson, in the shape of the Constitution of the United States of America.[1] The nation whose 200th anniversary we are called upon to celebrate in 1988 was founded just one year later. That would make it the first completely modern nation.

This view of Australia may put quite a strain on our credulity: did the convicts know they were coming to found a nation? Did they want to? Do the descendants of the Aborigines who saw the First Fleet land see things that way? Was a nation founded at all? After all, our monarch still lives overseas; many of our basic institutions are imported from our former Imperial ruler. If so, when was it founded? In 1788, in 1901, with the Statute of Westminster in 1928, or when appeals to the Privy Council were abolished in the mid-1980s? But what is a nation anyway in a world in which crucial economic and political decisions are no longer made at the national level, especially for the smaller states?

This book will attempt to grapple with some of the more significant recent attempts at making nationhood. In particular, it will focus on the conscious attempt to define the Australian nation as multicultural. The expression was first used in a public and official way by Al Grassby, as Immigration Minister of the Whitlam Government in 1973. The policy was elaborated by various government advisory bodies, in which the sociologist Jerzy Zubrzycki played a leading role, and was adopted by the Fraser Government. Its social policy consequences were mapped out in the Galbally Report of 1978. By the end of the 1970s multiculturalism had become not only a new Australian word, but also a full-blown 'ism': a comprehensive ideology of what Australia was supposed to be and to become. The policy was taken over by the Hawke Government and the state governments, and continues, despite some controversy, to enjoy the support of all major political forces.

Multiculturalism as an ideology calls for a celebration of cultural diversity as a continuing feature of Australian society.[2] It thus appears as a departure from previously prevailing racist and nationalistic stereotypes of the nation. But this progressive move bears problems: how is the tension between ethnic pluralism and the cohesiveness of society as a whole to be resolved? How can a nation be defined, if not in terms of ethnic identity: shared history, traditions, culture and language? How are core values and acceptable behavioural forms to be laid down, if the dominance of Anglo-Australian culture is no longer accepted? The problems of a multi-ethnic state are neither new nor unique in the world, but the response of multiculturalism is certainly a new departure in the history of Australia. So we must ask what multiculturalism means, and if it is a viable way of defining the nation.

But we must also ask if it is to be taken at face value. Has it really changed the ethnocentric structures which are so entrenched in every area of Australian life? Is it even meant to? It is also seen by some as a form of social control, a way of incorporating ethnic middle classes into the Australian political system, and using them to control their less successful compatriots, at a low cost to the state.[3]

The year 200 is a good moment to discuss attempts to define the nation, for the most obvious of these attempts is the Bicentennial itself. The Bicentennial Authority has been working for nearly a decade to:

> . . . plan, co-ordinate and promote a year long programme of local, national and international activities and events to celebrate Australia's Bicentenary and to involve 16 million Australians in the celebrations and events of 1988.[4]

As a planned, state-run exercise in the creation of a national idea, the Bicentenary is almost without precedent: for a whole year we are called upon to 'join in the activities of 1988 and to celebrate what it means to be Australian'.[5]

The Bicentenary is to be multicultural. We are told that 'Australians will really be "Living Together" in 1988'. The Bicentennial Authority has developed a 'set of planning objectives' to achieve this:

> To celebrate the richness of diversity of Australians, their traditions and the freedoms which they enjoy.

> To encourage all Australians to understand and preserve their heritage, recognize the multicultural nature of modern Australia, and look to the future with confidence.

> To ensure that all Australians participate in, or have access to, the activities of 1988, so that the Bicentenary will be a truly national programme in both character and geographic spread.[6]

There we have it: we must be multicultural to be national. And how shall we do it? The Authority tells us:

> Plant shrubs, hedges and trees . . . make community litter
> bags . . . Re-enact an episode from your district's past . . . Make
> a census of the headstones . . . Organize an Australiana Trivial
> Pursuit Game . . . Bake an Australia-shaped cake for a raffle . . .
> Plan to have a meal from a different culture at least once a month
> in 1988 . . . Paint a giant Bicentennial Living Together sign . . .[7]

But whatever you do, don't remind the public of unpleasant realities.
In 1987, the Bicentennial Authority asked Franca Arena, a NSW
State Labor MP, and Justice Michael Kirby, President of the NSW
Court of Appeal, to write articles for its glossy journal *Bicentenary
1988*. Arena wrote of migrants' encounters with 'racists, bigots and
intolerant people', and called for Australia to become a republic,
since the monarchy was meaningless for many Australians. Justice
Kirby described the unjust destruction and discriminatory impact of
the legal system on Aboriginal culture, and drew attention to concern
about the disproportionate number of Aborigines in jail. Their articles were rejected. Our image of multicultural Australia is meant to
be at the level of Trivial Pursuits: song and dance, food and folklore.

The Bicentennial itself is likely to be forgotten soon enough. It is
one of history's more extended one-night stands. But it is also part of
a long tradition of attempts to define Australia, and what it means to
be Australian. Why is there such a need to do this? Donald Horne
has pointed to the process of 'reality-creation' required to establish
new nation states:

> There are many characteristics a new nation-state might be seen as
> having. Only some of them prevail. In the processes that precede
> the formation of new nation-states great acts of imaginative con-
> struction occur, out of which the new nation is born.[8]

There is no doubt that the creation of a national ideology is part of
the political process of establishing the nation. The question of
which national characteristics prevail depends on the balance of
social forces within this process. Those who have the power to create
and rule a nation-state have the most influence in defining the
'national character'. The definition may embody abstract ideals
(liberty-equality-fraternity) and it might satisfy a popular desire to
'belong', but it is linked just as much to the economic and political
interests of the definers.

Now, if we are to follow Anderson, we all belong to 'new nations',
for all modern nations are a product of the last two centuries, being
closely linked to the economic and political processes of world
development.[9] Nor is the 'reality creation' of the national character
something that happens once, at the beginning of a new nation.[10]
Rather, there is a constant process of asserting, questioning, redefining and examining the national identity. As Horne writes:

> The great drama, endlessly playing, is that of maintaining defini-
> tions of the nation and its social order: definitions are being
> repeated daily, hourly, of what the nation and society are.[11]

So Australia's definers are doing what those of all nations do, when they put forward a national image. But they seem to do it with more regularity and fervour. Richard White starts his book *Inventing Australia* by calling it 'the history of a national obsession'. He points out that 'Australia has long supported a whole industry of image-makers to tell us what we are'.[12] White does not tell us why Australia should be a forerunner in this field. We may speculate that the cause lies in some of the ambiguities of the Australian condition. In seizing what they called empty land, the colonists denied the humanity of their Aboriginal predecessors' very existence. For the white invaders, there was no history before 1788. Thus Australian nationalism had to start from a year zero, or it has to regard itself as part of the history of the 'British race'.[13] Australia grew as part of the British Empire. Unlike the USA, India or Britain's other far-flung possessions, Australia never managed a decent independence movement, let alone a liberation struggle. Australia was made a nation by an Act of the British Parliament in 1901. The creation of a nation in a struggle for independence is usually the pre-eminent moment for the definition of national character, language, culture and myths. Australia has missed out on this, and has therefore had to make a more conscious effort to define itself. The task has not been made easier by its geographical position. On the other side of the world from its 'mother country' and sitting on the edge of Asia, the maintenance of Britishness put a strain on resourcefulness and imagination, especially as Britain's economy has faded and its Empire has crumbled.

White has documented the changing attempts to define the 'Australian type': the muscular sunburnt bushman, the 'Coming Man', whose self-reliance and physical prowess would renew the British race, the Digger, who proved himself at Gallipoli, the Bondi lifesaver:

> The emphasis was on masculinity, and on masculine friendships and team-work, or 'mateship' in Australia. All the clichés — man of action, white man, manliness, the common man, war as a test of manhood — were not sexist for nothing. Women were excluded from the image of the 'Coming Man', and so were excluded from the image of the Australian type as well.[14]

Being Australian has always been defined in sexist terms. It has also been defined in racist terms. In the early days, the pioneers' battle against the hard land was also seen as a struggle against the 'dangerous and wily' blacks. Later the fight was against migrants who would dilute the British character of the nation, and undermine the race. The main threat was the 'yellow peril' and above all the Chinese who started coming in the mid-nineteenth century. But there was hostility towards all 'non-Britishers'. One of the first Acts of the new parliament in 1901 was to pass the Immigration Restriction Act, designed to keep out non-European immigrants, and popularly known as the White Australia Policy. Humphrey McQueen has drawn attention to the role of racism in the construction of the Australian labour movement.[15] The restriction of immigration and the call for a white Australia were themes which had mobilized workers and their organizations — the unions and the Australian Labor Party in the latter half of the nineteenth century and which would continue to do so until the Second World War.

The Immigration Restriction Act was not generally used to keep out European settlers, although they were relatively few in number until 1947. Those who did come encountered considerable hostility. Australian workers were often unwilling to work with them. In the isolationist mood of the Depression era, attempts were made to exclude non-British migrants, and to combat their influence on other cultures within Australia. At Kalgoorlie in 1934 several people were killed in 'anti-dago' riots.[16] Attempts by employers to employ new migrants at low wages or to recruit them as strikebreakers did not help.

So the Australian type was constructed in terms of the white, masculine, outdoor person originating from the British Isles. Even that was contradictory enough in the light of the struggles between English and Irish. These came to a head during the First World War in the context of the Irish fight for independence and the conflict on conscription in Australia. The concept 'Anglo-Celtic', commonly used in debates on multiculturalism today, is an ill-conceived monstrosity, which can only partially paper over the gulf. One of the problems of defining the Australian nation is that its supposed substratum — the British nation — does not exist either. There is indeed a British nation-state, but it uneasily embraces four nations (or principal ethnic groups).[17]

There is, however, another side to the Australian type which was being constructed before 1945. The muscular bushman/digger/lifesaver was working-class. He was a 'battler' who did not take kindly to authority. It was a populist image that fitted into the concept of Australia as a 'workers' paradise' where there were no aristocrats, where there was no entrenched privilege, where everyone had a chance of success. This side of the Australian type is summed up in the ideas of 'mateship' and a 'fair go'.

How realistic was the image? From the earliest days of European settlement there was a strong measure of inequality in Australia. A landed oligarchy developed rapidly, and later merged with trading and manufacturing interests. There were class struggles throughout the nineteenth century, with the high demand for labour in the boom following the Gold Rush giving impetus to labour organization. The wealthier classes' demand for immigrant workers, and the existing working-class fear of dilution of labour, were central political themes for much of the nineteenth century.[18] Contrary to ideas of the open frontier and individualism, the state played a central role in

This is too confusing? Try "deny genocide & exclusionism..."

A NATION WITHOUT NATIONALISM? 9

Australian development. First it was the British Imperial state, later the governments of the states and the Commonwealth, but always there was a high degree of bureaucratic control. The idea of the individualistic bushman is clearly ambiguous. On the one hand it was an attempt to assert populist values against the ruling class and the state. On the other, it was an officially propagated image, useful to conceal the reality of a highly stratified, bureaucratized and increasingly urbanized society. Crocodile Dundee has had many predecessors.

Australia's self-image, therefore, has always been problematic. It has been racist, justifying genocide and exclusionism, and denying the role of non-British migrants. It has been sexist, ignoring the role of women in national development, and justifying their subordinate position. It has idealized the role of the 'common man' in a situation of growing inequality and increasingly rigid class divisions. It has been misleading in its attempts to create a British/Australian ethnicity while ignoring the divisions within the British nation-state, and its Australian off-shoot.

But for all that, the image might have been maintained had it not been for Australia's post-war immigration programme. We will argue in this book that the mass settlement of migrants from a wide range of countries has made the overt maintenance of a racist definition of the nation and of the Australian type impossible. Today an attempt is being made to re-interpret the immigration programme as a deliberate move towards a multi-ethnic society. That is far from the truth: immigration was seen in the mid-1940s as a strategic necessity to make the country economically and militarily strong enough to repel the 'yellow peril'. No ethnic diversity was intended: British migrants were wanted, and when they could not be obtained in adequate numbers, the call was for 'assimilable types' who would rapidly become indistinguishable from other Australians.

But, as will be shown below, cultural assimilation did not take place. Australia became a country with at least eighty different ethnic groups. Non-English speaking migrants and their children make up about one-fifth of the population. If the idea of a nation and of a national type is needed to secure social cohesion, then Australia is faced with a new problem: how to define these in a non-racist and non-monocultural way.

According to Ernest Gellner:

> . . . nationalism is a theory of political legitimacy, which requires that ethnic boundaries should not cut across political ones, and in particular, that ethnic boundaries within a given state . . . should not separate the power-holders from the rest.[19]

In other words, nationalism is based on the idea that every ethnic group or nation should have its own state, with all the appropriate trappings: flag, army, Olympic team and postage stamps. People relate to these symbols. A feeling of nation-ness is an integral part of their lived experience. But what happens when the people of a nation-state consist of more than one ethnic group, with different symbols and lived experiences? This is a common enough situation, but in the nationalist view of the world, it is likely to lead to conflict. As soon as people become conscious of their destiny as a nation they will either subjugate the other ethnic groups within the state boundaries, or, if they belong to a minority, they will fight for their own state.

Pre-industrial states, including the greatest empires, were held together not by national feeling but by a system of power, symbolized by the divinely-appointed monarch. For a colonial subject, loyalty to the British Crown had nothing to do with ethnicity. The modern nation-state, in its ideal form as a democratic republic, cannot exist on this basis. Since power belongs to the people, and is only delegated to the state (in its classical triad of legislative, executive, judicative), legitimacy cannot rest on loyalty to the state. The state is an instrument of the people; being loyal to it is a tautology. Legitimacy is based on the will of the people, and that makes it imperative to know clearly who constitutes the people: 'Nationalism is primarily a political principle, which holds that the political and national unit should be congruent.'[20] The struggles to make the state and the nation congruent have been at the root of much of the slaughter of our century.

Gellner

But what is a nation? It is not identical with a 'race' (whatever that is), nor simply reducible to an ethnic group. Yet the distinction is not clear:

Gellner

> . . . Communities which have been called national at one point of time or in one country, have been called ethnic and/or racial at others. While each collectivity has to be analysed in an historically specific manner, what is common to them all, in all their diversity, is that all are forms of ideological constructs which divide people into collectivities or communities . . . This involves exclusionary/inclusionary boundaries which form the collectivity, dividing the world into 'Us' and 'Them'. Although the constructs are ideological, they involve real material practices and therefore have material origins and effects. The boundaries of such collectivities tend to focus around a myth . . . of a common origin or a common fate, so that membership of the collectivity is normally obtained through birth. The boundaries of such collectivities can shift — they can cross-cut, expand or shrink in specific historical and socio-psychological situations, nor are they always symmetrical . . .[21]

non seq?

In fact there are very few countries today which are ethnically homogeneous. The process of industrialization and modernization leads to larger state units, embracing a variety of ethnic groups.

There are few advanced countries without their 'old' minorities such as the Bretons in France, the Basques and Catalans in Spain. Sometimes this develops into serious cleavage as in Italy and, increasingly, in Britain. Moreover, the process of development almost always involves rural-urban migrations which quickly transcend national boundaries: in the nineteenth century the Irish went to Britain, the Poles to Germany, the Italians to France and Switzerland, and people from all over Europe to the USA, Canada, and some South American countries. Since 1945 there has been large-scale labour migration to most Western European countries, to North America and Australia, leading to the development of significant new ethnic minorities throughout the First World.

In encouraging labour migration, the states concerned followed short-term labour market interests, with little consideration of the long-term consequences. There was certainly no desire to create multi-ethnic societies. Now that this has happened, there are various responses: *laisser-faire*, state racism or exclusionism, assimilationism, and multiculturalism. Whatever policy is followed, a new situation has to be dealt with: membership of the collectivity is no longer simply a result of birth; the boundary of the collectivity cannot easily be defined according to a myth of common origin or fate. If nationalism is a crucial social ideology then a new way must be found to define the nation. Nowhere is this problem more pressing than in Australia where the post-war migrations have been so large in scale that they have transformed the ethnic composition of the population. Forty per cent of the Australian people today are immigrants or children of immigrants. Half of these are of non-British origin.

Sixty years ago, J. Lyng could write:

> The position can be compared with that of a river, started by a small spring in the mountains, winding its way through unknown country, gaining in volume and importance as it flows along, till, at the end of its course, it has become a mighty stream with incalculable potentialities. Here and there the river is made slightly bigger by tributaries.[22]

The river was 'English language', 'English culture' and 'British stock' (an interesting juxtaposition). The tributaries were the most 'modest contributions' of 'non-Britishers'. Even in the 1950s it was possible to assert:

> Our life is still British wholecloth, so to speak, and though the warp-threads may have turned a little, they are still strong; we have only coloured and arranged the weft-threads a little differently.[23]

With hindsight, we can say that such a view of the world was ethnocentric and mistaken even then. But it did provide a workable basis for a national ideology.

That ideology could not survive the fundamental changes resulting from the crumbling of the British Empire, the post-war immigration programme and increasing vocal claims by Aboriginal groups. What were the alternatives? Other new, immigrant nations have had to contend with this problem. So have the new post-colonial nations of Africa and Asia, where it has been necessary to find a legitimation for political frontiers set up by imperialist powers, quite unrelated to previous ethnic boundaries. It is easy to understand the concepts that can hold the USA together without recourse to ethnic identity: they include the revolutionary tradition, the force of new universalistic ideals, the strength of the 'American way of life', the fascination of world power, the integrative force of modernism and innovation. Australia can aspire to such ideals only in an imitative, second-rate way. As Richard White has pointed out, in the 1950s attempts to define the nation focused on 'the Australian way of life'. The image was one of a prosperous suburban society, in which every man had his house and garden, his Holden and his hobby. Again, it was a sexist image, centred around the man as bread winner for a neat and happy nuclear family.[24]

It was a new image, that could compete with increasingly irrelevant Anglocentric traditions. And it could draw in the New Australians: you did not have to come from Britain to want a Holden and a house, to be a good worker and trade unionist, and to support the idea of a fair go. Consumerism matched the idea of assimilationism: to be Australian meant simply to conform in terms of work and lifestyle. The ideology of 'the Australian way of life' appeared as the pinnacle of modernism: pride in economic progress, technical advance and a high standard of living was to make differences in origin, race and ethnic background meaningless.

But by the 1970s, this approach was failing, and there was a need for a new national ideology. There were several reasons for this. First, the modernist, assimilationist principle had only scratched the surface of a society still highly elitist and dominated by Anglocentric values. Second, the onset of recession and restructuring of the world economy was making Australian living standards vulnerable. Third, trends towards economic and social segmentation linked to race, ethnicity and gender were making the whole concept of the 'Australian way of life' questionable. The idea of 'multiculturalism' was an attempt to modify existing concepts of the nation to match up to the new realities.

Whitlam's Minister of Immigration, Al Grassby, announced his version of a 'multi-cultural society of the future' in 1973. The ALP Government made efforts to take account of 'migrant needs' in its social policies. Fraser's neo-conservative Government took up the slogan, and by the end of the decade had worked multiculturalism up into a full-blown ideology for the Australian nation. Multiculturalism has been embraced by the Hawke Government and the various state governments, and remains a multi-party concensus. It has been questioned, recently, both through the old-style racist populism of Geoffrey Blainey and Bruce Ruxton, and through the strange New Right slogan of 'Anglomorphy'. But multiculturalism retains considerable power as an ideology because it does reflect important realities in Australia's social and cultural situation. For all its problems and contradictions it is unlikely that multiculturalism will be abandoned in favour of a return to Anglo-Australian ethnocentrism. It is currently the dominant discourse in the attempt to define the nation, and is likely to remain so for some time. Multiculturalism has become a necessary ideology.

Multiculturalism is progressive because it attempts to define the nation in non-nationalistic, non-ethnocentric terms. It is regressive because in some of its guises it often trivializes more serious social issues of inequality, founded in socio-economic structures, gender relations and structural racism. Its affirmative celebration of being colourfully different is a frequent cloak for deep-seated racism, for the continuing exclusion of Aborigines from Australian society, for the hardships of immigration, for the virtual exclusion of women from structures of economic and political power.

Multiculturalism is regressive for a second reason: it does not question the need to define the nation and to draw boundaries of inclusion and exclusion. By celebrating diversity within the nation, it reaffirms, even if often only in a perfunctory way, the need for a national cohesion which is more than that of the face-to-face community and less than that of all humanity. The step beyond multiculturalism is the transcending of national identity, the denial of its necessity, the recognition that through the crisis of modernity we are now all in the same boat — economically, ecologically and politically. Human identity must become transnational.

Plan of the book

Chapter Two is concerned with the way various groups, defined on racial or ethnic lines, have been incorporated or excluded from the larger structure of Australian society. A brief look at politics and attitudes towards Aborigines, non-Europeans and European immigrants in the pre-1945 period is followed by a description of the situation of Aborigines in the labour market today. We then examine the post-war immigration programme, and its impact on Australian society. We describe a labour market segmented by racial/ethnic divisions and gender, and then look at current changes in a period of economic restructuring.

Chapter Three describes and discusses the policies and ideologies developed to manage the incorporation of immigrants into the Australian economy from 1947 until the emergence of multiculturalism in the 1970s. Chapter Four continues the story, analysing the changing meaning and content of multiculturalism as an ideology and a guide to social policy up to the present.

Chapter Five provides a brief international survey, looking at the way immigrants have been incorporated in Western Europe and North America, and what consequences this has had for ideologies of people and nation. The period of economic recession and restructuring has been marked by a resurgence of racism in many developed countries.

Chapter Six deals with theories of nationalism, racism, ethnicity and culture, in the context of Australian history. We show how such theories have been used to underpin changing concepts of what we are and should be, and how these concepts relate to economic and political interests.

Chapter Seven examines in detail the development of multiculturalism as an ideology, and shows how it is linked to a conveniently restricted understanding of culture. The publicly accepted concept of culture is narrowed down to a safe, static and marketable commodity, which often amounts to a trivialization of actual living processes.

In Chapter Eight we raise some fundamental questions on Australia's future. We briefly discuss possible alternatives to the construction of national identity, in a late industrial First World country.

Notes

1. Benedict Anderson, 'Narrating the nation', in *Times Literary Supplement* 13 June 1986.
2. Multiculturalism has other meanings too, which will be discussed later in this book.
3. Andrew Jakubowicz, 'State and ethnicity: multiculturalism as ideology', in: J.Jupp (ed.), *Ethnic Politics in Australia*, Sydney: George Allen & Unwin 1984.
4. Australian Bicentennial Authority, *Fact Sheet*.
5. Australian Bicentennial Authority, *How to Make it Your Bicentenary*, 1987.
6. *How to Make it Your Bicentenary.*
7. *How to Make it Your Bicentenary.*
8. Donald Horne, *The Public Culture*, London and Sydney: Pluto Press 1986, p.8.
9. This theory is developed in Benedict Anderson, *Imagined Communities*, London: Verso 1983. See also: Ernest Gellner, *Nations and Nationalism*, Oxford: Basil Blackwell 1983.
10. Although the idea is tempting: The French National Convention decided to restart history, by declaring the year of the abolition of the monarchy as year one of a new calendar, as Anderson points out in: 'Narrating the Nation'.
11. Horne, p.21.
12. Richard White, *Inventing Australia*, Sydney: George Allen & Unwin 1981, p.viii.

13. '. . . it may be said that to all intents and purposes, the history of the British in this country is the history of Australia'. J.Lyng, *Non-Britishers in Australia*, Melbourne: University Press 1939, p.1.

14. White, *Inventing Australia*, p.83.

15. Humphrey McQueen, *A New Britannia*, Ringwood Victoria: Penguin 1970.

16. White, p.146.

17. See Tom Nairn, *The Break-up of Britain*, London: Verso 1981.

18. Marie de Lepervanche, 'Australian immigrants 1788-1940', in: E. L. Wheelwright & K. Buckley, (eds), *Essays in the Political Economy of Australian Capitalism*, Vol. 1, Sydney: ANZ Book Company 1975.

19. Gellner, *Nations and Nationalism*, p.1.

20. Gellner, p.1.

21. Nira Yuval-Davis, 'Ethnic/racial divisions and the nation in Britain and Australia', *Capital and Class* 28/1986, p.92.

22. J. Lyng, *Non-Britishers in Australia*, p.1.

23. W. E. H.Stanner, 'The Australian Way of Life', in: W. V. Aughterson (ed.) *Taking Stock*, Melbourne: Cheshire 1958, p.8.

24. White, Ch.10.

2.

Racial/Ethnic Divisions and Social Structure in Australia

Colonialism and migration

Racial and ethnic divisions have played a central role in the shaping of the Australian labour force since 1788. Racism and the utilization of migrant labour have been crucial factors in the history of the Australian economy and cultural identity both in the colonial era and since. Social conflicts around these questions have helped shape Australia's political institutions and cultural life.

The analysis of these factors is complicated, for we are dealing with two distinct, though interlocking, processes: the first is the colonial land grab, which dispossessed the Aboriginal people, and which was based on physical and cultural genocide. The second is the process of labour recruitment, migration and settlement, necessary to provide a workforce for an emerging industrial society. The first process is one of destruction and partial exclusion from the developing society; the second is one of incorporation. Although the state (first the British state, later those of the colonies and then the Commonwealth and the states) has played a central role in both processes, the military, economic, legal and ideological mechanisms involved are different in quality.

A full historical analysis of these twin processes of genocide/exclusion and recruitment/incorporation is not possible here. This chapter will concentrate on the current situation, rather than on the past. Some of the historical dynamics of the use of unfree labour will be discussed in an international-comparative way in Chapter Five. The development of ideas on racism and identity in response to these processes will be discussed in Chapter Six. Here we will merely raise a few issues which are central to understanding the current situation.

Why did colonial policy centre on the destruction of the Aborigines, with very little effort to incorporate them even as unfree labour? If we look at the impact of colonialism on other indigenous peoples throughout the world, we might advance tentatively the proposition that policies depended to some extent on the economic system of the conquered people: European settlers set out to destroy the material basis of hunter-gatherer societies, and often to exterminate such peoples. This applies to the North American Indians, the Caribs, the San peoples of Southern Africa as well as the Australian Aborigines. On the other hand, where indigenous peoples were sedentary agriculturalists, colonialism aimed to incorporate them into the economy and society. Often this meant integrating them into the colonial economy and even using their political structures (for example, using traditional chiefs as colonial officials). This applies to many areas of Africa, Asia and Latin America, and to the Maori in New Zealand.

The reason for this is fairly obvious: the use of extensive areas of land by hunter-gatherers stood in the way of colonial agriculture, and did not produce surpluses which could be expropriated and exported. Clearing the land for cattle, sheep and plantations meant destroying the indigenous peoples' subsistence basis, and led to conflict and — in view of European superiority in weapons technology — genocide. The more thickly populated areas of pre-colonial agriculturalists, on the other hand, provided both directly exploitable commodity resources, and large pools of labour, suitable for plantations and fundamental infrastructural projects. This is not to say that one form of colonialism was in any way socially or morally superior to the other: the horrors of forced labour in the Belgian Congo rivalled Auschwitz. But, obviously, there is a limit to the extermination practised by the second type of colonialism, for no one wants to destroy a source of useful labour.[1]

British colonialism in Australia had an interest in denying the very existence of the Aborigines as human people. The fiction of 'the empty land' provided a basis for legal justification of white usurpation. The very real resistance of Aboriginal people to colonization was omitted from the official histories of settlement. Aborigines were defined as non-persons, who had no state, no recognizable form of society, no culture. They were labelled by racist theories as inferior pre-humans: full-blooded Aboriginals were expected to die out in competition with the superior 'Nordic' white race, while 'half-castes' might gradually be absorbed.[2] Denied their traditional means of subsistence and kept subservient by rations and alcohol, the fate of the Aborigines seemed clear, in a racist self-fulfilling prophecy:

> Little by little they lose their energy, virility, and whatever racial pride they once possessed; they become indolent and apathetic towards life . . .[3]

This was no basis for their incorporation into the economy as wage workers. Nonetheless, with the ending of the convict labour system in 1840, some attempts were made to recruit Aborigines as cheap labour for the pastoralists, for few free white men wanted the hard and lonely job of shepherding.[4] The incorporation was never more than marginal: in 1926 it was estimated that the number of Aborigines in European employ in the whole of Australia was something over 10,000.[5]

So, for a variety of reasons, Aborigines were not a significant source of labour for colonial Australia. Labour had to be brought in from overseas, initially from Britain. The first form of labour was the forced labour of convicts, who carried out the vital task of creating basic economic infrastructures, under the harshest of conditions. This made possible a rapid expansion of the pastoral industry from the 1820s, leading to a demand for additional free labour. British migrants were recruited on a large scale by both government and private agencies. Assisted migration was seen as a way of alleviating poverty in Britain, just as transportation remained a way of getting rid not only of criminals, but also of working-class radicals, such as Chartists and trade unionists. The destitute poor of Britain's workhouses did not prove a good source of labour for Australia's pastoralists, and there were complaints both from employers and from urban workers who found the new migrants a source of competition and a threat to conditions. Australian working-class opposition to immigration, which later gave rise to racism and xenophobia, started with mistrust for new British migrants, even though these were later incorporated into the working class and the labour movement.[6]

The gold rushes of the 1850s led to a huge influx of new migrants, many of them from other European countries. The Australian population doubled in a decade, reaching about one million in 1861. Prior to 1850 there had been some Germans, mainly in South Australia, and some Jews. Some Chinese had been recruited as indentured labourers prior to the gold rushes. Now large numbers of Chinese came in as gold-diggers. The rapid arrival of this exclusively male population led to fears of economic competition, and to racist prophecies of the dire effects on scarce white womanhood. The result was anti-Chinese riots, and the introduction of measures for taxing and excluding the Chinese in NSW and Victoria. Since British Imperial policy called for free movement of labour within the Empire, demands for Australian Federation, democracy and independence came to be associated with racial exclusion and the protection of labour.[7]

Soon racist propaganda was extended to cover the recruitment of Indians and South Pacific Islanders by Queensland plantation owners. Hughes, the Labor Party's leader in 1901, considered that

> our chief plank is, of course, a White Australia. There is no compromise about that! The industrious coloured brother has to go — and remain away.[8]

The new Commonwealth Parliament passed the Immigration Restriction Act in 1901, establishing the White Australia Policy, which was to remain in force as the basis for immigration policy until the late 1960s.

Another significant ethnic division was that between the English and the Irish. Many of the earliest convicts were of Irish extraction. The Great Famine of 1845 led to a mass exodus of Irish to Britain, the USA and Australia. The wretched situation of the Irish made them a potential threat to wages and conditions. Moreover, the virulent anti-Irish racism prevalent in Britain at the time was transplanted to Australia. Although Irish people did not, on the whole, form separate communities, the division between them and the English continued to split the working class, coming to a head during the First World War when the Easter Rebellion in Ireland inflamed feelings, and the Irish in Australia led the anti-conscription movement.

Migration continued at a high level until about 1890. Much of it was from Britain, but there were also Germans, Italians, Scandinavians, Greeks, Lebanese and others. Immigration was not restricted, so most came of their own accord, but there were also assisted migrants. Some attempts were made to recruit foreign indentured labourers, such as Italians for the Queensland plantations, to replace the South Pacific Islanders, who were repatriated after racist agitation. There seems to have been a high degree of racism and discrimination against Southern Europeans. However, as Marie de Lepervanche points out, there were also divisions among people of British origin:

> Although many of these British immigrants eventually became absorbed into the Australian wage-earning fraternity, and protested in turn against arrivals more recent than themselves, there remained a continual cleavage in the working class at this time between colonial worker and British assisted immigrant. In short, the employers' search for cheaper and more abundant labour, and consequently their advocacy of assisted immigration, divided colonial worker from potential British competitor.[9]

This helps indicate the semi-rational genesis of working-class hostility towards immigration. To the extent that employers used immigrants to attack wages and conditions, labour opposition is understandable, and is to be found even where there is no racial or ethnic difference. But, all too easily, this defensive behaviour becomes transmuted into the ideology of racism.

Between 1891 and 1945, immigration was at much lower levels than before, and consisted mainly of people from Britain. Apart from a brief expansionary period in the 1920s which did lead to substantial — often assisted — immigration, economic growth was slow, and the demand for labour low. By 1947 Australia had the lowest proportion of overseas-born (9.8 per cent) ever recorded for the non-

Aboriginal populations. Many observers see this as a period in which increasing homogeneity provided the conditions for a growing sense of Australian nationhood, articulated by groups like the Australian Natives Association or the Returned Services League. This national feeling was based on 'White Australia' and opposition to non-British immigration, but also a feeling that Australia was better than Britain, and 'Pommy' migrants should feel privileged.[10]

However, there was some Southern European immigration, particularly from Italy and Greece in the 1920s. Many of the Italians went into agriculture in Queensland. The Southern Europeans encountered considerable hostility. There were bomb outrages against Italians, who had been used as strikebreakers on Melbourne wharves. In 1930, two shiploads of Italians were refused permission to land. In 1934 there were 'anti-dago' riots at Kalgoorlie, in which several people were killed.[11] Various laws were passed to limit the rights of non-British immigrants. The most restrictive were those in Queensland, where foreigners' employment was restricted in the banana and sugar industries, in dairy produce premises and in the working of tramway and omnibus services. Land ownership was also made subject to special conditions.[12] This was a period of widespread and virulent racism against Southern Europeans. Again, the hostility was based in part on their success as competitors for jobs, or as farmers under difficult conditions.

This brief summary should be sufficient to indicate the complexity of patterns of incorporation of different groups into the growing Australian economy and society. Apart from the Aborigines, there was no rigid system of exclusion. Rather, different migrant groups, including those from Britain, were incorporated in varying ways at different times. Established workers tended to see migrants as competitors who would take their jobs and erode their hard-won rights. Many employers indeed encouraged immigration, and supported assisted passage schemes for this very reason. Migration was a constant focus of social conflict, and racism became a deep-seated feature of Australian ideology and culture.

Aborigines: marginalization and exclusion

At the time of the 1981 Census, the Aboriginal and Torres Strait Islander population, enumerated on the basis of self-assessment, was estimated to be around 171,000 or about 1.2 per cent of Australia's total population.[13] The results of the 1986 Census indicate a substantial increase in Aboriginal population, presumably because changing consciousness has made Aborigines more willing to declare their origins.

By the 1930s, it had already become clear that the Aborigines were not going to 'die out' as had earlier been supposed, and there was a shift to a policy of assimilation: Aborigines were expected to lose their identity in the wider community. In fact, this has not happened. The Aboriginal population remains to a large extent both culturally differentiated and structurally excluded in economic, social and political terms.

Until the 1960s, the policy of assimilationism was a cloak for concealing the desperate socio-economic situation of many blacks, both urban and rural. Lack of special provision meant ignoring the enormous problems created by an epoch of genocide, cultural imperialism, sexual exploitation and paternalism. Moreover, successive governments systematically attempted to destroy Aboriginal identity: families were broken up through removal of children to 'training camps' or white foster parents. This continued into the 1950s, with Australia increasingly coming to be compared with South Africa. In 1967 a referendum established that Aborigines would be counted as citizens, with the right to vote. The McMahon Government established a Council for Aboriginal Affairs which began funding incorporated Aboriginal groups. A rising tide of political action by Aborigines put land rights on the political agenda. In 1972 the Whitlam Government set up a Department of Aboriginal Affairs, taking over most of the state powers in this area (with the exception of Queensland). The Commonwealth Aboriginal Land Rights Act (NT) was passed in 1976, despite the change to a more conservative government under Fraser. It had an important impact on popular consciousness, although its scope was confined to the Northern Territory. But by the early 1980s the Commonwealth Government was in retreat from earlier promises, in the face of pressure from the powerful mining companies.[14]

We will not go into the complexities of these political developments here. The campaign by mining interests and their New Right friends has had important ideological effects. An attempt has been made to portray the Land Rights movement as a divisive force, creating a sort of 'apartheid in reverse', by dividing Australia into black and white areas. So the fight of Aborigines for the restitution of some small part of the land taken from them has become an issue in the ideological offensive against multiculturalism. We will look at this in Chapter Seven. Here we will merely describe the economic and social situation of Aborigines.

There is a lack of precise information on Aborigines' economic position. Even the most comprehensive piece of research — E.K. Fisk's study of *The Aboriginal Economy* — gives no breakdown by occupation nor industry, nor any exact figures on unemployment. The general picture one gets is that Aborigines are still for the most part not integrated in the mainstream economy nor the social life of the nation. Fisk speaks of an 'Aboriginal sector' in the Australian economy.[15] He divides the Aboriginal population into four groups: outstation dwellers (about 5 per cent of all Aborigines), residents of

Aboriginal towns (20 per cent), those living in smaller non-Aboriginal towns, often in 'fringe-dweller camps' (34 per cent), and those living in cities (41 per cent). A high proportion of these Aborigines who are in work are employed by government: 39 per cent of employed Aborigines, compared with 24 per cent of all Australians. A recent survey of Aboriginal work in Victoria, the Aboriginal Labour Force Analysis (ALFA), found that 60 per cent of Aboriginals in employment worked for Aboriginal organizations, and a further 23 per cent worked for government departments.[16]

Fisk finds that Census and other data on unemployment did not give an accurate picture, but that 'unemployment among Aborigines is very much higher than amongst the population as a whole'.[17] Whitfield, on the other hand, quotes Census data indicating Aboriginal unemployment of 9 per cent in 1971 (compared with 1 per cent for the whole population), 19 per cent in 1976 (compared with 5 per cent) and 25 per cent in 1981 (compared with 6 per cent). Aboriginal youth unemployment in rural areas is as high as 90 per cent.[18] About two-thirds of the ALFA sample in Victoria were not employed, but seeking work. The most recent study, by Dr Russell Ross of the University of Sydney, puts Aboriginal unemployment in NSW at 75 per cent for men, and 60 per cent for women. Fisk suggests that the main reason for high unemployment is not racial discrimination, but Aborigines' lack of education, skill and experience at a time when structural factors are leading to a decline in unskilled jobs. By early 1987 only 18 Aborigines had ever obtained higher degrees, and 112 had achieved Bachelor degrees. From 1971 to 1981, an average of 35 Aborigines per year obtained trade certificates. The school retention rate (the proportion of students staying on from Year 8 to Year 12) was only 11 per cent for Aborigines in 1983.[19] This deplorable educational situation is itself a product of racial discrimination and exclusion. Another problem is location: Aboriginal settlements have not arisen out of economic considerations, but as a result of past patterns of welfare administration. Problems are most severe in the 'fringe-dweller camps' on the outskirts of country towns.[20]

The result is that most Aborigines have incomes well below the national average, depending on welfare payments, or on poorly-paid casual work. In the 1981 Census, only 1 per cent of Aborigines and 3 per cent of Torres Strait Islanders reported incomes over $15,000 per year, compared with 14 per cent of the white population. Only 17 per cent of Aborigines had incomes above $8,000 compared with 44 per cent of all Australians. The consequence is that large proportions of the Aboriginal population live in poverty, although Fisk does suggest that some outstation dwellers may be somewhat better off, as they can supplement their income by hunting.[21] In 1983 the infant mortality rate for Aborigines was 3.6 times the national average.[22]

Many Aborigines are victims of a vicious cycle of deprivation, in which racial discrimination, together with lack of education and training, cause unemployment, which in turn leads to poor housing and health, alcohol and drug abuse, and a general situation of hopelessness. Children brought up in such circumstances easily become caught in the same trap.

To sum up, it appears that no real effort has been made to incorporate Aborigines into the Australian labour force in the period of post-war expansion. Nor have over twenty years of citizenship brought much improvement in social and economic conditions. There has been some discussion of the merits of bringing Aborigines into the labour force, as a partial alternative to immigration, and some degree of incorporation has taken place in the pastoral industries of the outback.[23] But on the whole the effort has not seemed worthwhile to employers and governments: the Aboriginal population is seen as too small to make a major contribution to meeting large-scale labour demands, and the political and economic costs of overcoming the effects of generations of white racism are too high. Despite rhetoric on participation and equal opportunity, official responses to the situation of the Aboriginal population are still defined in terms of welfare and policing.

Migrant workers: incorporation and segmentation

The period following the Second World War was marked by rapid expansion and structural change in the Australian economy. The long post-war boom throughout the First World, together with the strengthening and restructuring of industry during the War, provided favourable conditions. The aim was not only growth, but also the establishment of a national manufacturing sector to reduce dependence on primary industries. This led to a strong need for additional labour, which could not be met by natural population growth, nor by haphazard spontaneous immigration. So, in 1945, the Department of Immigration was set up, under Arthur Calwell, to initiate a programme of large-scale labour immigration. The aim was 1 per cent population growth per year through immigration.[24]

In view of traditional working-class suspicion of immigration, an ideological justification for the programme was needed. It was found in the appealing slogan of 'populate or perish', which played on wartime fears of Japanese invasion, and resurrected the image of the 'yellow peril'. There was certainly no desire to create a multi-ethnic society. At first the aim was to attract British immigrants. When they could not be persuaded to come in sufficient numbers, 'racially acceptable' Eastern and Northern Europeans were recruited, and the public was told that they would be fully assimilated as 'New Australians'.

Immigration was an economic success: from 1947 to 1973 it provided 50 per cent of labour force growth, giving Australia the highest rate of increase of any OECD country. The Department of Immigration in many cases deliberately sought out low-skilled workers for recruitment. As newcomers lacking language proficiency, often without industrial experience and qualifications, the migrants provided a source of labour for unskilled and semi-skilled jobs. Often discrimination and non-recognition of qualifications forced even highly-skilled migrants into manual manufacturing jobs. In the early years, many migrants were admitted only on the condition that they would live in camps and work where directed for two years. So, in the 1950s, German, Dutch, Italian and Baltic migrants:

> provided an easily directed, mobile reserve army to overcome the bottleneck areas of building and construction, heavy industry and public utilities. These migrants made up more than 70 per cent of the extra workers needed in the steel industry and over half the workforce on the Snowy Mountain Scheme.[25]

Labour migration helped to increase the size of the working class, and to restructure it. Bringing in new workers at the bottom of the labour market gave Australian-born workers the opportunity of upward mobility. Immigrant workers appeared, in the early stages, to be separate from the Australian working class. Widespread racism against 'dagos', 'refos' and 'wogs' deepened the split. The use of cheap migrant labour seemed to benefit all Australians by improving the infrastructure and increasing manufacturing output. It also led to a larger domestic market, which was crucial to the growth of manufacturing industries.

So immigration was the motor of post-war expansion, right up to the beginning of the period of recession and stagnation in the 1970s when the Whitlam Government cut immigration targets substantially. They crept up again under Fraser, with a shift in emphasis to entries of refugees and to the implementation of a family reunion policy. The Hawke Government has maintained this emphasis, though most recently there has been new significance given to the economic desirability of immigration, and immigration levels have again been increased. This is not the place to chart the intricacies of immigration policies.[26] What is significant for the purposes of the present work is the way post-war immigration has changed the structure of the Australian population and labour force.

As we have noted when the post-war immigration programme started in 1947 Australia had a higher proportion of Australian-born citizens than ever before: about 90 per cent. This was because immigration had been low in the years of economic crisis between the wars. About 8 per cent had been born in the British Isles (or other

English speaking countries) and only about 2 per cent came from non-English speaking countries. Population doubled from 7.5 million in 1947 to about 16 million at present. More than half the increase was due to immigration and to births to immigrant parents within Australia.

Today, two out of every ten Australians are first-generation immigrants, while another two out of every ten are children of immigrants (the 'second generation'). Moreover, through the post-war years, the proportion coming from Britain and Ireland has declined, with increasing numbers being recruited at first from Northern and Eastern Europe, then from Southern Europe, and later from the Middle East, Asia and the South Pacific. By 1981 only 37 per cent of the foreign-born population were from Britain and Ireland, while a further 37 per cent were from Europe, 3 per cent from the Middle East, 3 per cent from Africa, 3 per cent from America, 7 per cent from Oceania and 8 per cent from Asia.[27] Since 1981[28] the trend towards increased immigration from non-European areas has continued, as Australian wages and living standards have declined compared to the rest of the developed world. The British are still the largest single nationality among new entrants, but they are followed now by Vietnamese and South Africans.

The Australian population is one of the most ethnically diverse in the world, with about 100 ethnic groups, speaking some 80 immigrant languages and 150 Aboriginal languages.[29] In August 1985, 1.7 million overseas-born persons were in employment in Australia. The 622,000 migrant women made up 24 per cent of the total female labour force, while migrant men were 26 per cent of the total male labour force.[30] These figures are for first generation migrants only. If children of migrants were added, almost half the total labour force would be the result of the post-war migrations. The largest number of foreign-born workers are from the UK and Ireland (615,300), followed by Italy (153,400), New Zealand (111,700), Yugoslavia (83,800), Greece (81,100), Germany (66,000), Netherlands (54,700) and Vietnam (35,700). The vast majority are from Europe (72 per cent) followed by Asia (13.7 per cent) and Oceania (7.6 per cent). At present there is a slight decline in the number of European-born workers, as the migrants of the 1950s and 1960s reach retiring age, while their Australian-born children enter the labour force. The Asian share of the labour force is increasing slowly. But the main shift in the labour market is the dramatic increase in female employment: 10.6 per cent from 1981 to 1985. This trend affects both Australian and foreign-born women, and is to a large extent due to the growth of part-time employment.

As already pointed out, migrants have not simply provided additional labour. Rather, they have been mainly incorporated into particular positions within the urban, manual, manufacturing working class. In Melbourne, for example, the 1981 Census showed that 51 per cent of all workers in manufacturing and 39 per cent in construction were overseas born.[31] The Australian labour force is highly segmented. In other words, there is a strong link between place of birth, gender and the types of job people are likely to get. Segmentation means that job opportunities are based not just on a person's work ability, qualifications and productivity, but also on non-economic ascriptive criteria, linked to ideologies of gender, race and ethnicity. Labour markets are structured to place women, migrants and racial minorities at a disadvantage, and their low-status positions are in turn taken as practical proof of innate inferiority.

In Australia, migrant origin alone is not a criterion for segmentation: British migrants and many of those from Northern Europe do as well on average (and sometimes better) than the Australian-born. To illustrate the point, Table 2.1 summarizes the occupational status[32] of men and women by birthplace for two occupational groups: a high status white-collar category, and the principal manual work category. It can be seen that men and women from English-speaking countries from Germany and from Asia[33] have representation in the Professional/Technical and Related Services category roughly similar to the Australian-born. People from Italy, Yugoslavia and Lebanon are considerably under-represented. When we look at the Tradesmen/Production/Labourers category, Southern Europeans and Lebanese are considerably over-represented. This applies most particularly to women: only 6.1 per cent of Australian-born women are in this category, compared with 42.2 per cent of Greeks, 33.7 per cent of Italians, 33.3 per cent of Lebanese and 48.9 per cent of Yugoslavs.

These data indicate a very high concentration of both men and women from Southern Europe and the Middle East in manual occupations, and a corresponding under-representation in the higher status white-collar jobs. Altogether there is considerable disparity between the occupational status of non-English speaking (NES) background migrants and the rest of the labour force.

We find similar evidence of labour market segmentation when we look at data by industry, rather than occupation. For example, one study indicates that one-third of the Australian-born population in Melbourne are employed in manufacturing and construction, compared with over half of the overseas-born population. Birthplace groups with particularly high concentrations in manufacturing and construction are Greeks (57 per cent), Maltese (58 per cent), Italians (57 per cent), Yugoslavs (70 per cent), Turks (75 per cent) and Latin Americans (58 per cent). These groups were considerably under-represented in the Finance and Community Service industry groups. When these data are related to information on occupation it is found that:

Table 2.1   Selected occupational status categories by birthplace, Australia 1981 (per cent)

	Men		Women	
	Cat. 0	Cat. 7/8	Cat. 0	Cat. 7/8
Australia	11.9	37.0	18.0	6.1
New Zealand	13.2	42.9	17.2	7.9
UK/Eire	13.8	42.4	17.3	8.9
Germany	12.2	49.8	15.3	12.5
Greece	n.a.	n.a.	2.7	42.2
Italy	3.7	59.4	3.5	33.7
Lebanon	2.3	56.4	2.7	33.3
Poland	10.0	56.7	12.7	23.0
Yugoslavia	3.1	73.0	4.2	48.9
Europe NEI	12.2	51.1	15.5	17.8
Asia NEI	18.8	38.5	19.3	22.6
America	21.3	38.5	25.4	14.7
Total overseas born	11.1	45.8	13.8	17.8
Total	11.7	39.5	17.0	9.1

Source: Census 1981, adapted from Des Storer, *Migrant Workers in Victoria-Trends in Employment and Segmentation*, Melbourne: Victorian Ethnic Affairs Commission Working Paper 5, 1985.

Notes: Cat. 0   = Professional/Technical and Related Services
         Cat. 7/8 = Tradesmen/Production/Labourers
         n.a.   = not available
         NEI   = Not elsewhere indicated

not only do migrants from non-English speaking countries concentrate in Melbourne's manufacturing and construction industries, but also they tend to concentrate almost exclusively in category 7/8 jobs, working as production workers/labourers within these industries.[34]

Australian-born workers, or migrants from English-speaking countries employed in manufacturing are far likely to be in professional, administrative or clerical jobs than NES workers.

Migrant workers from NES countries — particularly from Southern Europe, the Middle East and South East Asia — are overwhelmingly manual workers in manufacturing and construction. This in turn leads to lower incomes and higher unemployment for these groups. Migrant disadvantage is even greater when account is taken of factors not visible to official figures. Poor working conditions, unhealthy working environments, industrial accidents and illness, outwork, informal sector employment and hidden unemployment are all factors which tend to affect non-English speaking migrants more than other workers.

It is often argued that migrant disadvantage affects new migrants. transitorily. In time they should adapt to Australian conditions and do as well as anyone else. The data we have presented on the occupational and industrial distribution of migrant workers do not substantiate this view. In his analysis of the Victorian labour market, Des Storer has examined the experiences of NES background migrants arriving at different periods. He shows that they have tended towards increasing concentration in manufacturing and construction: those who arrived in the 1950s entered a labour market with developing manufacturing industries, but still significant small businesses and agricultural enterprises. Less than 50 per cent of them entered manufacturing and construction. By contrast, those arriving in the late 1960s and through the 1970s went overwhelmingly into manufacturing and construction (Over 90 per cent of NES background migrants). Storer's data indicate that migrants of the 1950s experienced some mobility, but later entrants have overwhelmingly remained in production jobs.[35]

Moreover, segmentation in employment patterns has been matched by concentration into certain geographical areas. Migrants have gone where expanding industries needed them, and this has overwhelmingly been in the industrial suburbs around the big cities (especially Sydney and Melbourne) or in expanding towns based on specific industries (Newcastle, Wollongong, Whyalla, Geelong, etc.). The 1981 Census showed that 80 per cent of overseas-born persons lived in major urban areas (defined as cities with 100,000 or more inhabitants) compared with 59 per cent of the Australianborn. The concentration was most marked for persons from Southern Europe, the Middle East and Vietnam.[36]

NESB migrants' concentration in low status jobs affects their earning power. In August 1985, the average weekly earnings for Australian-born males was $392. In comparison, men from Greece earned an average $334, from Italy $363 and from Yugoslavia $351. Australian-born women earned an average $304, compared with $273 for women from Greece, $265 for women from Italy and $269 for women from Yugoslavia.[37] We lack comparable figures for people from the Middle East and South-East Asia, but in view of their concentration in manual occupations, there can be little doubt that their earnings are well below average. A similar picture emerges when we look at household incomes. Figures from the 1981 Census indicate that Greek families had average incomes of $12,159 and Italians of $13,129 compared with the average of $14,182 for the Australian-born. In other words, Greeks were on average 15.1 per cent worse off and Italians 8.3 per cent worse off.

So there can be little doubt that certain migrant groups are at a disadvantage in terms of income, and that this factor is increased by gender discrimination: migrant women workers from Southern Europe, the Middle East and South-East Asia are likely to be in the lowest income groups. Additionally, it must be stressed that official Census and labour market statistics never give the full picture. As manufacturing has declined, migrants lacking English language proficiency, education and training have been forced out of regular employment into the informal sector or 'black economy'. They often work in insecure and undocumented jobs as 'self-employed' builders, casual workers in catering or retailing, or as outworkers. Such workers often have extremely low incomes, invisible to official statistics. A study by the Trans-National Co-operative documents actual hourly wages of $3 or even less for women outworkers.[38]

Economic restructuring and unemployment

Much has been made of dramatic stories of migrant success. Here is an example of the way this popular perception is cultivated:

He's wealthy, flamboyant and has a taste for expensive cars, boats and aircraft and he's coming to Wollongong. Queensland's hairdressing tycoon Stefan Ackerie is ready to curl in our city . . . He has 75 salons through the country and the latest will open in the new Crown Gateway shopping centre on October 20 . . . The Lebanese-born hair stylist has made it through hard work and a determination to succeed at whatever he turns his hand to. A better than average golfer, barefoot skier, boxer and a kung fu expert, the barber of the north is a man of many talents . . . His early days in Australia were spent in Longreach and Maryborough in Queensland where he re-affirmed his belief that if you give a little extra and charge no more you'll succeed. He originally learned the lesson washing cars as a child in Lebanon. 'I always put a flower on the dash of each car', he said. 'So I got all the cars to wash because I added the flower. It's the same today.' (*Illawarra Mercury*, 27 August 1986)

Yet such 'ethnic entrepreneurs' are far from typical. Labour market segmentation and concentration into certain areas may not have appeared as a problem as long as manufacturing was growing. But when the recession started to bite in the 1970s and the early 1980s it was the manufacturing industries and areas which had developed in the boom, which now bore the brunt of restructuring. The Kirby Report on labour market programmes in 1985 pointed out:

The greatest falls (in employment) have been concentrated in the processing and assembling sectors in manufacturing. This has important implications for the future employment opportunities of low-skilled people, particularly non-English speaking migrants.[39]

At the peak of its development in 1973, Australian manufacturing employed nearly 1.4 million persons. By 1983 manufacturing had declined by 248,600 jobs. During the same period a net total of 449,700 new jobs were created in the economy as a whole. The big growth sector was Community Services with 381,200 new jobs.[40] Despite the growth in jobs, unemployment rose substantially as increasing numbers of school-leavers and more women entered the labour force. What were the chances of getting the new jobs for NES background migrants? A recent government report describes the following situation for New South Wales:

A major factor affecting migrant unemployment in New South Wales is the location of concentrations of migrant/ethnic groups within Sydney. The inner-city areas have suffered major job losses, particularly in manufacturing industries in the past ten years. Traditionally these areas have been major sites of first settlement for newly-arrived immigrants, many of whom then moved to other suburbs when they became economically established. Immigrants who remained in these areas are generally those who had not achieved any degree of socio-economic mobility. This leads to concentrations of immigrants who are more likely to be vulnerable in areas where there has been an erosion of the employment base. Similarly, economic and structural factors have led to a marked erosion of the employment base in Wollongong, which also has an above-average concentration of immigrants from non-English speaking countries. The location of three of Sydney's four migrant centres in the south-west has also led to a heavy concentration of immigrants, particularly the newly-arrived, in an area with a very limited employment base. A similar situation is evident in most other states.[41]

There are many migrant success stories in Australia, but that does not contradict the fact that large numbers of migrants have become 'locked into' low-skilled work in manufacturing, and have remained in the industrial suburbs where they first settled. In the boom period, the incentive to move out of such jobs may not have been very great, as they offered reasonable wages. But as such jobs have declined, many migrants have found themselves out on a limb: they have not obtained the education, training and language proficiency needed to compete for the new jobs in community services or other white-collar areas.

Some people seek a solution in setting up small-scale businesses, or becoming self-employed. The result is a growth of marginal small enterprises, which often fail, leaving the instigators heavily in debt. Others succeed, but only at the price of a high degree of self-exploitation — extremely long working hours at low rates of return, often for the whole family. Many migrants, especially women, are formally self-employed, but are in fact highly dependent on exploitative work relationships as outworkers.[42] Many older migrant workers retrenched from industry withdraw from the workforce altogether, due to lack of realistic employment prospects, or poor health. They, too, do not appear in unemployment figures.

Unemployment has increased for all sections of the population since the early 1970s in Australia. Everywhere it has been groups over-represented in low-skilled and low-status labour market segments which have borne the brunt of restructuring: Aborigines, immigrants from Southern Europe and the Middle East and South-East Asian refugees. Generally, the women in these groups have been hit even harder than the men. Unemployment rates for both male and female migrants have been higher than for the Australian-born throughout the 1980s — generally by about 10 to 25 per cent. The gap has tended to widen in the most severe recession periods, such as 1982-4. Recent migrants have fared worst: those resident in Australia less than twenty months have had unemployment rates three to four times higher than the Australian norm.[43]

However, these aggregate figures are misleading, for they conceal important differences between the various birthplace groups. Some had unemployment rates lower than or similar to the rate for the Australian-born (8.7 per cent in March 1987): people from the UK and Ireland 7.7 per cent; from Italy 7.1 per cent; from Greece 4.9 per cent. Other groups had somewhat higher rates: people from Yugoslavia 10.7 per cent; from Germany 10 per cent; from New Zealand 9.6 per cent. Extremely high rates of unemployment were suffered by the Lebanese (36.9 per cent) and the Vietnamese (34.3 per cent).[44]

Clearly there are important differences in the situation of various migrant groups: length of residence, age structure (older persons tend to have lower unemployment rates), language proficiency, education and skills, occupational structure, and so on. Migrant youth in particular have disturbingly high rates of unemployment, as was shown by one of the last studies carried out by the Australian Institute for Multicultural Affairs, before it was abolished by the Federal Government in July 1986. AIMA found that the development of youth unemployment has paralleled that of adults, but at consistently much higher levels. The gap between rates of adult and youth unemployment increased considerably during the recession. Teenagers (15-19) have been particularly affected, with an average unemployment rate of 22.3 per cent in 1984. The rate of unemployment for overseas-born youth is considerably higher than for the Australian-born. In 1984, 26.5 per cent of overseas-born 15-19 year olds were unemployed, compared with 21.7 per cent of Australian-born in that age group. Of overseas-born 20-24 year olds, 17.1 per cent were unemployed compared with 12.1 per cent of Australian-born 20-24 year olds.

The highest rates of youth unemployment are to be found in the inner cities (which are also the areas of highest migrant concentration). Again it is the youth of non-English speaking background who are most affected, so that in certain areas rates of 30 per cent or more out of work may be found. High youth unemployment is also found in outer suburban areas where housing is relatively cheap but where job prospects and transport are poor.

Forecasts on the likely development of youth unemployment carried out by the Institute of Applied Economic and Social Research for AIMA indicate the disturbing prospect that around one-third of overseas-born teenagers and one-fifth to a quarter of overseas-born young adults are likely to be out of work in the future.[45] The social consequences for those inner-city communities where unemployment is concentrated are likely to be devastating.

As we have already noted, statistics on unemployment never give the full picture. There are always a large number of 'hidden unemployed': people who want to work, yet fail to satisfy the job-seeking or availability for work criteria, and are therefore not officially classified as unemployed. For obvious reasons, we can only guess at the number of hidden unemployed — some estimates put it at the same level as the number of persons officially regarded as unemployed. Women are particularly affected, as their lack of employment can be masked by an unwilling withdrawal into household duties. NES background immigrants are particularly affected, as language difficulties, lack of understanding of bureaucratic procedures and despair at the prospect of getting employment discourage registration with the Commonwealth Employment Service. There is no doubt that NES background migrants, and particularly migrant women, are a majority of the hidden unemployed.[46]

The migrant workers who came to Australia prior to the mid-1970s were crucial to the expansion of manufacturing. Now many of them are bearing the brunt of the decline in this sector. The restructuring of the world economy has affected the Australian labour market in several ways. First, Australian and transnational companies now have much of their labour-intensive production carried out in low-wage countries, in Asia or Latin America, for example. This has helped reduce jobs in Australian manufacturing. Second, Australian manufacturers have been able to increase pressure on their employees to take wage cuts, to accept poorer conditions, and to speed up work. Third, there has been a drive for more 'flexible' forms of work, in which large companies contract out jobs to small firms, and to out-workers, leading to highly exploitative and insecure forms of employment, especially for women. Fourth, the concentration of financial and management functions in 'world cities' like Sydney leads to a high demand for construction and personal services, to meet the needs of an élite of highly-qualified personnel. This need is often met by 'ethnic' small businesses (such as restaurants, boutiques, delicatessens), which are competitive through a high degree of utilization of unpaid family labour. Fifth, the large corporations in the 'world cities' attract qualified staff from less developed areas, reinforcing the 'brain drain', particularly from Asian countries.

Many of the migrants of the post-war boom period today remain as marginal workers in sectors threatened by decline and retrenchment. Others have already been forced out, to join the ranks of the long-term unemployed. Here they are joined by the Middle East and South-East Asian migrants of the late 1970s and early 1980s, who entered the labour market at a time when there were few low-skilled jobs to be had. Forced to the periphery of the labour market, these groups form a labour reserve for capital. Marginal workers who become marginal entrepreneurs often do so without any gain in living standards or security. At the same time, employers and government encourage new immigration, especially of people with capital or marketable qualifications. This is seen as crucial for the reshaping and modernization of the Australian economy.

Social mobility

Many migrant workers have paid a high price for participation in the Australian Dream: hard, dangerous and dirty work, long hours, poor health. Many have returned disillusioned to their country of origin, or have simply dropped out of the labour force and become isolated and impoverished in Australia. But a lot of migrants have been successful, saving enough to purchase a house and consumer durables. In some cases there has been upward social mobility: migrants have been able to move out of manual work in manufacturing and gain higher status white-collar jobs, or set up successful businesses.

Some people argue that the difficulties of the immigrants themselves do not matter in the long run. They may indeed be regarded as a 'lost generation', but a major motivation for migration, it is argued, is 'a better life for the children'. On this basis, Australia has kept its promise to migrants, if their children can climb out of manual work and enter the middle class. Recently, a lot of effort has been put into showing that this is happening.

For instance, Bob Birrell and Anne Seitz have examined studies of the educational experience of Sydney high school students[47], data from the 1981 Census on school retention rates and occupational mobility, and on the ethnic background of university students. They find that children of 'ethnic origin' (i.e. children of NES background migrants) are staying on at school longer, and doing better than students of Australian-born parents. They claim that 'ethnic disadvantage' is a myth, and that there is considerable intergenerational mobility: the children of migrant manual workers are moving into white-collar jobs. By contrast, they find that the children of Australian blue-collar workers are not doing as well at school, nor entering tertiary education, so that most remain within the manual working class.[48]

Brian Bullivant comes to very similar conclusions on the basis of a study of seven Melbourne high schools. He argues that there is an 'aspiration-motivation gradient':

> At the top are significant numbers of Asian students . . . Most Anglo-Australian students from middle to high SES (Social Economic Status) homes are close to this top group. A few rank at the top with the Asian students. Next . . . are students from NES backgrounds, especially Greeks, Yugoslavs and Italians. Next again and lower on the gradient are other ethnic groups, especially those from Northern Europe and Britain together with significant numbers of Anglo-Australian students, especially those from middle-to-low SES areas.[49]

The reason for the apparent success of migrants' children, according to Bullivant, is the 'ethnic work ethic'. They are therefore no longer the disadvantaged at school.

> Instead it is highly probable that significant numbers of Anglo-Australian students are at risk of becoming a new category, namely, the self-deprived, in the sense of inhibiting their own life possibilities and career scenarios . . . What can be termed the self-deprivation syndrome is a cluster of traits. They include students' own lackadaisical attitudes towards the value of education and dis-inclination to work hard to achieve their goals. It also appears to be due to lack of parental encouragement and drive, which in contrast are so apparent among parents from NES and Asian background . . . It may not be stretching matters too far to suggest that most of these aspects form part of the general Anglo-Australian value system.[50]

Similarly, Birrell and Seitz attribute the alleged success of migrants' children to the strong traditions of 'family solidarity and discipline' in most of the NES background ethnic groups. This gives students the right motivation and attitudes for success in an Australian school system based on 'equality and meritocracy'. Australian working-class children, by contrast, are held back by a class culture which prompts 'an oppositionist unco-operative stance towards teachers and school authorities'.[51]

The consequences of these findings are clear: 'ethnic' students are doing very well, so there is no need for special English language, multicultural or other educational programmes. The problem lies with the 'self-deprived' Anglo children, who need to improve their attitudes. This fits in very well with current New Right ideologies, with their emphasis on strong family discipline, and the importance of having competitive and uncritical attitudes towards work and authority. The idea is that the labour market offers equal opportunity to anyone willing to work, and that there is no need for state intervention to combat social disadvantage.

How valid are such findings on the inter-generational mobility of people of non-English speaking background?[52] To start with, staying on at school a long time does not always imply educational success. Birrell and Seitz present figures calculated from the 1981 Census on school retention rates for 15-19 year olds. These indicate that sons and daughters of Greeks, Italians and Yugoslavs are more likely to stay on till year 12 than sons and daughters of Australian-born people.[53] But migrants' children living in declining manufacturing areas often stay on at school because there is little chance of a job if they leave. High school retention rates may be a form of concealed unemployment. Moreover, those who have been held back in early years due to language problems often stay on longer to get minimum school-leaving credentials.[54]

Census figures on the occupations of children of migrants have been taken to indicate a high degree of upward mobility, compared with their parents. But it should be remembered that many migrants have actually experienced downward mobility when entering the Australian labour market. Many who were self-employed, professional, or white-collar workers in their countries of origin, have become manual workers in Australia, because of language difficulties and unrecognized qualifications. So in some cases the upward mobility of the second generation represents a return to the previous status of their parents.

Wood and Hugo have carried out a detailed analysis of the 1981 Census data, noting considerable evidence of inter-generational mobility from manual occupations towards higher status white-collar employment. For instance, 11.6 per cent of Australian-born people with Greek parents have Professional and Technical occupations compared with 1.5 per cent of the first generation. For Italians, the comparable figures are 10 and 3.4 per cent, for Yugoslavs 13.2 and 3.2 per cent, and for those from the Middle East 12.7 and 2.7 per cent. Correspondingly, far fewer members of the second generation are in the category Tradesmen, Process and Production Workers. However, complete comparability has not been achieved: the proportion of second generation persons of Southern European and Middle East origin in the high status Professional and Technical occupations is still lower than that of children of Australian-born. There are high proportions of Greeks and Italians in clerical occupations, indicating that inter-generational mobility has been mainly from blue-collar to the bottom end of the white-collar hierarchy.[55] This is not surprising: in recent years, as children of migrants have entered the labour market, there have been relatively few blue-collar jobs available. The growth has been in low-level white-collar jobs.[56] The 1981 Census also indicated that members of the second generation had rates of unemployment considerably higher than those of the migrant generation, but also higher than those of young people whose parents were Australian-born.

To sum up, there is substantial inter-generational mobility of children of NES migrants. Many have done well in the education system, and have achieved high occupational status. On the other hand, many children of migrants are encountering great difficulties at school, are finding it hard to enter the labour market, and have high rates of unemployment. Rather than a general trend towards upward mobility, we seem to be witnessing a polarization within and between migrant communities into those who do fairly well, and those who remain disadvantaged.

Race, ethnicity and socio-economic position

Australia has long prided itself on being able to offer a high living standard to its working people. The working class and the various groups who make up the middle class have enjoyed high earnings, and have been able to afford house ownership, possession of cars and other consumer durables, and the life-style that belongs to the Australian dream. Apart from the extremes — the millionaires and the millions below the poverty line — it is this broad spectrum of reasonable prosperity which has determined the ideology of Australia as a classless society. But in the 1980s, the very rich have increased in numbers and power while the real wages and living standards of the working population have fallen. Indeed, many constantly risk joining the growing ranks of the unemployed, the marginalized and the impoverished.

What has been the impact of post-war immigration on Australian social structure? What are the implications of the current social and economic situation? We have argued above that the labour force is segmented according to racial/ethnic and gender divisions. This is neither new nor unique: such criteria have played a significant part ever since colonization. Similarly, racial/ethnic and gender divisions are to be found in all contemporary societies. A worker's income, working conditions and job security depend not only on his or her economic characteristics (education, training, productivity, etc.) but on ascriptive factors linked with race, ethnicity, citizenship and gender. The use of such 'irrational' criteria appears to contradict the principle of the free market, but in fact has historically been a major strategy for dividing and controlling the labour force.

There is no fundamental difference between race and ethnicity: both are socially constructed markers used to regulate group boundaries, defining who is to be included and who excluded from a given collectivity. There is nothing objective about such categories: they are the product of social processes. The way race and ethnicity have been constructed in Australia will be discussed in more detail in Chapters Six and Seven.

Race has, on the whole, been used as a more absolute marker for exclusion than ethnicity. It has generally been applied to non-whites — either the Aboriginal population, or Asian and Pacific Islander immigrants. Racist ideologies and practices against Aborigines started with a policy of genocide, shifted later to an attempt at forced assimilation, and more recently to a partial political recognition of the need for separate policies. The result has been a situation of non-incorporation of most of the Aboriginal population into Australian society. Although a minority have working-class jobs, and an even smaller group have obtained middle-class positions (generally through government Aboriginal affairs programmes), most have a marginalized position, marked by exclusion from the labour market, poverty and poor social conditions. Special legal, welfare and police systems have been set up for social control of Aborigines. Today, after more than twenty years of rhetoric on equity and participation, Aborigines are still the victims of structures of racial exclusion.

Racial categories were used in the nineteenth century to define the situation of Chinese, Indians and Kanakas. The White Australia Policy became a centrepiece of labour politics, and remained so until the 1960s. Yet, as we have seen, racism and exclusionism applied to white immigrants as well, if not in such an extreme form.

The information presented in this chapter makes it clear that we cannot speak of immigrants as a single or uniform socio-economic group. To start with, immigrants from some English-speaking countries and Northern Europe appear to be doing as well, and sometimes better, than the Australian-born. Secondly, even though certain birthplace groups (Southern Europeans, Middle East migrants, South-East Asian refugees) are not doing well on average, there are many individuals who have achieved upward mobility. There are no absolute ethnic or racial barriers in Australia, but there is marked segmentation: the great majority of high-status positions are held by white men, born in Australia, other English-speaking countries or Northern Europe. Other men and many women from these areas are mainly in middle-class occupations. Men from Southern Europe, the Middle East and South-East Asia are over-represented in manual worker occupations. Women from these areas are also over-represented in manual occupations, with on average even lower skill and income levels than the men.[57]

Immigrants have found their way into all social classes in Australia, inevitably perhaps, in a period of such dramatic demographic and economic growth. They have provided not only labour power, but also consumer demand, new ideas and impulses for change. The most significant impact of non-English speaking immigrants has been on the working class. In view of the racist ideologies of the Australian working class before 1945, and the support of the labour movement for the White Australia Policy, it is perhaps remarkable that the large scale incorporation of newcomers into this class should have taken place with comparatively little conflict. The main reason for this is that immigrant workers did not appear as a threat. They came in at the bottom of the labour market, causing upward mobility for Australians. Their presence contributed to a general improvement in prosperity. They were not used as strikebreakers or wage-cutters. They quickly took on a 'worker mentality', and joined the unions.[58]

There was hostility towards 'wogs', 'dagos' and 'refos' in the early stages of post-war immigration, and this is discussed in the following chapter, but it rarely led to open public conflict or exclusion. By the 1970s, the labour movement was ready to move away from the White Australia Policy. But the growth of non-European immigration — first from the Middle East, then from India, Malaya etc., and then the South-East Asian refugees — coincided with the end of the boom, and the escalation of unemployment. In these circumstances, there was every reason to fear a racialization of politics and the emergence of a racial split in the working class. Both Australian history and events in European countries (see Chapter Five) provided precedents. On the whole, this has not happened. The 'Blainey Debate' of 1984 seemed to herald such developments, but they have remained low-key. Racism may be just below the surface, but it has not (yet) re-emerged as a major political force. The trade unions' official move towards an anti-racist stand have transformed Australian labour attitudes, in comparison with an inglorious racist past.[59]

Australia clearly has a segmented labour market, with race, ethnic origin and gender playing a part in determining socio-economic position. But the working class is not so politically fragmented by racism as it was in the past, nor to the same extent as the working class in Britain and some other European countries at present. Labour migration has had a major impact on social structure in Australia in the post-war period. The main aspect of this has been economic: the vast influx of migrant labour helped to transform the Australian economy in the period of manufacturing expansion. There is a continued economic role for migrants in the current phase of restructuring. They bear a disproportionate share in the burden of unemployment. In addition, their flexibility in shifting into small, marginal businesses, outworking and sub-contracting helps reduce the cost of services for larger-scale enterprises. Migrants thus play an important part in the current process of decentralization and internationalization of production in certain industries.[60]

What are the future prospects for migrants in Australia? There is evidence of upward educational and occupational mobility of migrants' children. This may not be as general as some people think, but it is significant, and it means that the labour market function of the first generation will not altogether be inherited by the second generation. That is one reason why employers and the state put a high priority on continued immigration, despite relatively high unemployment levels.

If the children of migrants do not serve as a labour reserve, then new workers must be imported. But Australia's labour needs have changed. In the 1950s and 1960s, manufacturing needed docile and hard-working labourers, to replace Australians moving into the white-collar sector. Today the situation is more complex. The labour market is becoming polarized. On the one hand, the highly-organized and productive large enterprises (both corporate and public) require a well-qualified and suitably motivated workforce. As the Australian educational system is still unable to provide such workers in adequate numbers, immigration policy is used to provide a 'brain-drain' of trained personnel — increasingly from Asian countries. On the other hand, the demand for housing, services, and luxury consumer goods on the part of the upper and middle classes requires increasing numbers of low-skilled and exploitable workers: to build the houses, to staff the speciality restaurants, and to sew the boutique clothes. Here there is a need for migrant workers, whose situation forces them into low-status employment, frequently in the informal sector. The categories of new migrants who meet this need are often those who come under family reunion or refugee categories.

The celebration of the 'ethnic work ethic' is indicative of the role the new migrants are expected to fulfil, as intakes are once again raised. Employers hope that Asians, with their 'strong family discipline' and their 'correct attitudes' towards work and authority, will help to counteract what they see as the 'bloody-mindedness' of the Australian worker, who is obsessed with trade union solidarity and restrictive work practices, and the unco-operativeness of the Australian student, who lacks respect for teachers. Once again, immigration is meant to compensate for deficiencies in Australian education and social policy, and to allow growth without basic changes in structure and attitudes.

Notes

1. Compare C.D. Rowley, *Recovery*, Ringwood Victoria: Penguin 1986, p.17.
2. J. Lyng, *Non-Britishers in Australia*, Melbourne University Press 1935, pp.204-5.
3. J. Lyng, p.203.
4. Marie de Lepervanche, 'Australian immigrants 1788-1940', in: E.L. Wheelwright and K. Buckley (eds), *Essays in the Political Economy of Australian Capitalism*, Vol.1, Sydney: ANZ Book Company 1975, p.74.

5. J. Lyng, p.207.
6. de Lepervanche, p.76. See also J.Collins, 'The political economy of post-war migration', in: E.L. Wheelwright and K. Buckley (eds), *Essays in the Political Economy of Australian Capitalism*, Vol.1, Sydney: ANZ Book Company 1975.
7. J. Jupp, 'Australian immigration 1788-1973', in: F. Milne and P. Shergold (eds), *The Great Immigration Debate*, Sydney: Federation of Ethnic Community Councils of Australia 1984.
8. Quoted from J. Collins, p.107.
9. de Lepervanche, p.85.
10. J. Jupp, pp.8-9.
11. de Lepervanche, p.99.
12. de Lepervanche, p.98.
13. E.K. Fisk, *The Aboriginal Economy in Town and Country*, Sydney: George Allen & Unwin 1985, p.4. This figure is based on corrected estimates from the 1981 Census. Officially, the Aborigines are defined as those people, partly or wholly of Aboriginal descent, who identify themselves as Aborigines, and who are accepted as such by the community with which they identify.
14. C. D. Rowley, Chapters 2 and 3.
15. Fisk, p.1.
16. *ALFA: Major Findings and Recommendations*, Melbourne: Monash University 1987.
17. Fisk, p.11.
18. K. Whitfield, *The Australian Labour Market*, Sydney: Harper & Row 1987, p.117.
19. *Sydney Morning Herald*, 26 May 1987.
20. Fisk, pp.106-110.
21. Fisk, p.63 and p.105.
22. *Sydney Morning Herald*, 26 May 1987.
23. See Mervyn Hartwig, 'Capitalism and Aborigines', in: E.L. Wheelwright and K.Buckley (eds), *Essays in the Political Economy of Australian Capitalism*, Vol.3, Sydney: ANZ Book Company 1978.
24. Collins, p.108.
25. Collins, p.110.
26. J. Collins, *Migrant Hands in a Distant Land*, Sydney: Pluto Press 1988.
27. F. Milne and P. Shergold (eds), *The Great Immigration Debate*, Sydney: FECCA 1984, p. 142.
28. Most statistics referred to in this chapter are from the 1981 Census, which is the most recent comprehensive data source available. The results of the 1986 Census will not be available before the publication of this book. This presents difficulties, as the recession of the early 1980s led to considerable changes in the structure of the labour market.
29. Department of Immigration and Ethnic Affairs, *Don't Settle for Less — Report of the Committee for Stage 1 of the Review of Migrant and Multicultural Programs and Services*, Canberra: AGPS 1986, p.42.
30. Australian Bureau of Statistics (ABS), *The Labour Force* (Catalogue No. 6203.3).
31. D. Storer, *Migrant Workers in Victoria: Trends in Employment and*

Segmentation, Working Paper No.5, Melbourne: Victorian Ethnic Affairs Commission 1985.

32. Occupational status groups together various occupations thought to be on similar skill levels, but cutting across industries, e.g. a person could be a carpenter (skilled tradesman) in a variety of industries. Industry classifications put together all persons working in a certain industry, whatever their specific jobs or skill levels, e.g. someone working in the car industry could be a manager, a technician, or a manual worker.

33. The figure for Asia may appear somewhat surprising. The 1981 Census was taken before the major influx of refugees from Indochina, whose skill level was generally not high. However, most non-refugee Asian migrants have above-average skill levels.

34. Storer, p.21.

35. Storer, pp.26-35.

36. G. Hugo, *Changing Distribution and Age Structure of Birthplace Groups in Australia 1976-81*, Adelaide: National Institute of Labour Studies 1983, pp.21-2.

37. ABS, Weekly Earnings of Employees (Catalogue No.63100).

38. TNC Workers Research, *Anti-Union Employment Practices — Final Report*, Sydney: TNC 1985.

39. P.E.F. Kirby, *Report of the Committee of Inquiry into Labour Market Programs*, Canberra: AGPS 1985, p.42.

40. D. Storer, *Migrant Workers, Unemployment in Victoria: Trends and Policy Directions 1985*, Melbourne: Victorian Ethnic Affairs Commission 1985, p.11.

41. *Report of Commonwealth, State and Territory Ethnic Affairs Officers on Migrant Unemployment*, Melbourne: AIMA 1986; see also: R. Kriegler and J. Sloan, *Technological Change and Migrant Employment*, Adelaide: National Institute of Labour Studies 1984.

42. TNC Workers Research.

43. S. Castles and others, *Patterns of Disadvantage among the Overseas Born and their Children*, Wollongong: Centre for Multicultural Studies 1986, pp.30-33.

44. ABS, *The Labour Force Australia*, March 1987.

45. Australian Institute of Multicultural Affairs (AIMA), *Reducing the Risk, Unemployed Migrant Youth and Labour Market Programs*, Melbourne: AIMA 1985.

46. *Report of Commonwealth, State and Territory Ethnic Affairs Officers on Migrant Unemployment*.

47. J. Martin and P. Meade, *The Educational Experience of Sydney High School Students*, Report No.1, Canberra: AGPS 1979; P. Meade, *The Educational Experience of Sydney High School Students*, Report No.3, Canberra: AGPS 1983.

48. R. Birrell and A. Seitz, *The Ethnic Problem in Education: The Emergence and Definition of an Issue*, Paper from AIMA Conference, Melbourne 1986.

49. B. Bullivant, *Are Anglo-Australian Students becoming the New Self-Deprived in Comparison with Ethnics?*, Melbourne: Monash University 1986, p.22.

50. Bullivant, pp.22-23.

51. Birrell and Seitz.
52. For further similar findings see I.Burnley, 'Convergence or occupational and residential segmentation?' in: *Australia and New Zealand Journal of Sociology*, Vol.22, No.1 and N. Mistilis, *Destroying Myths: Second-Generation Australians' Educational Achievements*, Melbourne: Monash University 1986 (unpublished paper).
53. Birrell and Seitz, p.22.
54. M. Kalantzis and B. Cope, *Why We Need Multicultural Education: A review of the 'Ethnic Disadvantage' Debate, Wollongong*: Centre for Multicultural Studies 1987.
55. D. Wood and G. Hugo, *Distribution and Age Structure of the Australian Born with Overseas Born Parents*, Canberra: DIEA 1984.
56. One of the problems of examining changes in occupational status is that the work content and social status of specific occupational categories changes over time as the labour process develops and new forms of work organization are introduced. An occupation or category which was regarded as having high status twenty years ago may now have become proletarianized — something which has happened to office jobs as the result of new technology. Compare E. O. Wright and Singelmann, 'Proletarianization in the changing American class structure', *American Journal of Sociology*, Vol.88 Supplement.
57. Compare J. Collins, 'Immigration and class: the Australian experience', in: G. Bottomley and M. de Lepervanche (eds), *Ethnicity, Class and Gender in Australia,* Sydney: Allen & Unwin 1984, pp.11-21.
58. Constance Lever-Tracy and M.Quinlan, *Breaking Down the Barriers: Asian Immigrants and Australian Trade Unions*, Brisbane: Griffith University.
59. Lever-Tracey and Quinlan.
60. Compare R.Miles, 'Labour migration, racism and capital accumulation in Western Europe', in: *Capital and Class* 28 Spring 1986.

3.
Assimilation to Integration 1945-1972

Why multiculturalism?

This chapter is concerned with the public discourse on immigration at crucial periods during the years since 1945.[1] It concentrates to a great extent on politicians and bureaucrats, not in the belief that such people completely determine the content of national identity, but that they play a large part in so doing. In a stratified society, even one which is a liberal democracy, it is possible for an élite consensus to develop that is quite at odds with what the majority of the population would vote for if asked directly; and in the area of immigration we would argue that this has been the case more often than not.

Jean Martin saw the process of ideological production in this way:

> . . . part of the capacity to dominate the construction of public knowledge is the capacity to decide what will happen to new private knowledge or new social knowledge . . . whether it will be permitted to become public knowledge, and in what context, or whether it will be ignored or suppressed.[2]

We would certainly agree with this as far as it goes but we argue that public knowledge is constructed in circumstances generally not chosen by the constructors and from materials often little to their liking. In the present context the 'circumstances' of most importance have been defined by the economy in both its international and domestic aspects: and the 'materials' have included the surviving stock of past ideologies.

At the beginning of the post-war period the question of Australian national identity was not a contentious one. Effectively, Australians were portrayed as an offshoot of the British 'race' who had adapted the cultural tradition and the institutions of the British to antipodean conditions (generally by bettering them). The question of Aborigines was brushed aside with the doctrine of their impending disappearance and non-anglophone ethnic minorities were seen as tiny exotic enclaves, unassimilable and (as the wartime treatment of many of them demonstrates) potentially dangerous.

Forty years on, the question of national identity certainly is contentious. Both major parties espouse a policy of cultural pluralism within a framework of national cohesion, yet the limits of pluralism and the necessary degree of coherence are not only left vague but are issues continually picked over. The very idea of multiculturalism as a goal has been bitterly attacked by traditional populists such as Professor Geoffrey Blainey, by the dinosaurs of the Old Right such as Victorian RSL President Bruce Ruxton and by the janissaries of the New Right such as Professor Lauchlan Chipman and Frank Knopfelmacher. Many Aborigines have also attacked multiculturalism as it applies to them, vigorously asserting that the idea of the equal validity of all cultures in Australia simply reduces them to the status of just another ethnic minority. Sections of the political left have asserted that multiculturalism is basically a tactic to divert attention from structural inequality. Last and probably most important, many people whose main ancestry is from the British Isles would accept the goal of multiculturalism only in a restrictive context and in a permissive (as opposed to prescriptive) sense. People have a right to 'their own cultures' but the sphere of culture is limited to food, language and dress. Basic 'Australian' values are still defined in terms similar to those used in the mid-1940s; there is a deep suspicion of ethnic groups which are perceived as too tight-knit; and the very notion of 'special treatment' for individual ethnic groups is anathema.

We have, then, two main problems. First, why has multiculturalism emerged as a state ideology at all? Second, why is it that the elite consensus is different from the 'common sense' of the largest section of the population?

The most commonly accepted answers to these questions essentially centre around a process of increasing awareness of the consequences of mass multi-ethnic immigration and the role within this of a number of 'definers' of the migrant experience who include a range of community activists, social workers, bureaucrats and politicians. This process was certainly important, as is amply demonstrated by Jean Martin: but it does not occur in a vacuum. Both the tempo and direction of this process was determined by a number of background factors. Most important were: the changing internal structure and international standing of the Australian economy; the changing ethnic composition of the immigration intake; and the changing relations of Aboriginal Australians with *all* immigrant groups. In order to illustrate this process, we wish to examine several crucial periods. The early years of the immigration programme (the late 1940s and early 1950s) and the period of retreat from the White Australia Policy in the late 1960s will be dealt with in this chapter. In the following chapter, we will examine the turning points in the development of the ideology and policy of multiculturalism: the first phase in the Whitlam years, the development of cultural pluralism under Fraser, in particular through the Galbally Report, and finally the zig-zag course adopted in this area since the Hawke Government came to power in 1983.

Assimilation

For the entire period from the later 1940s to the mid-1960s migrants were allowed to present no threat whatsoever to a concept of national identity based firmly upon the supposedly shared British roots of the bulk of the population. Indeed, in a curious, even paradoxical, way the doctrine of assimilation, so vigorously espoused by the government of the period, did much to reinforce both the sense of homogeneity and the sense of superiority of the anglophone population.

Most obviously, the demand that migrants should assimilate quickly and totally to some supposedly 'Australian' culture implicitly asserted the superiority of this culture over that of the migrant. More subtly, the notion of a unified host culture papered over differences in cultural practice in this country linked to social class, gender or geographical (rural/urban) location, and also consigned to historical limbo sharp ethnic divisions which had existed before 1945. Most obviously and predictably there was nothing Aboriginal to which migrants were enjoined to assimilate. In addition, assimilation speeded the process by which the distinctive contribution of the Irish was so far erased from memory that it eventually become possible for otherwise literate people to describe whole sections of the Australian population as 'Anglo-Celtic'.

Assimilation had other important aspects: for an overt racist exclusivity based on the supposed superiority of certain racial-biological features, it substituted a covert racism based on the proposed incompatibility of certain cultures; and it drew the limiting line at which this incompatibility began, namely where a culture ceased to be 'European'. Thus the post-war years saw the joint operation of an immigration programme of unprecedented size and a White Australia Policy of unprecedented severity, bordering on fanaticism. The image of the 'European' as 'self' (or as capable of becoming such) and the 'Asian' as irrevocably 'other' was every day reinforced in public rhetoric and practice.

All of this is so familiar a part of our post-war history that we tend to take it as a 'natural' state of affairs, and forget that assimilation was far from being an obvious or unambiguous doctrine. To start with, it is hard to accept that people like Immigration Minister Calwell could sincerely have believed that a migrant intake of the size and diversity which came to Australia could readily be absorbed to the point of invisibility, particularly in view of the strength of nationalism and racism in Europe at the end of the Second World

War. Admittedly, the Department of Immigration sought academic advice from demographers (like Borrie and Price) and social psychologists (like Taft and Richardson) who were proponents of the assimilationist theories of immigration which had developed in the USA between the World Wars. But it is even harder to believe that government took almost two decades to become disabused of the expectation of assimilation.

Second, actual practices in recruitment and direction of labour brought about the segregation that official policies were meant to hinder. There is a contradiction between the expectation of cultural homogeneity, and labour market policies which brought about economic and social segmentation.

Third, the discussion on who could be regarded as 'assimilable types' raised damning questions. Why should people who had spent most of their conscious lives subject to fascist indoctrination, for example, be any more able to assimilate to Australian values than people from the Pacific region? The only conceivable answer is, because the former were white, but that makes nonsense of assimilationist dogma — the problem lay in the bigotry of the receiving population, not in the characteristics of the migrants.

Fourth, we must ask why assimilation was regarded as a desirable (or even possible) goal, at a time when other countries importing labour opted for temporary immigration and not assimilation: for example, the 'guest worker' systems of Switzerland and Belgium, and later West Germany.

The assimilationist/White Australia package had three essential ingredients, relating to the question of national identity:

- Australia was a culturally homogeneous society based on British values and institutions.
- This homogeneity would not be disturbed by mass European immigration.
- It could not survive any Asian immigration.

Why was there such enthusiasm for this problematic policy? In Chapter Two, we looked briefly at some of the motivations for the post-war immigration programme. Was the main aim to populate rather than perish, or to supply factory fodder?

The line of reasoning most often followed was the Keynesian link between high aggregate demand and high inflation, with wage drift being seen as a major link in the process by which demand pressure translated into price rises. For example, H. C. Coombs, wartime head of the Ministry of Postwar Reconstruction, describes in the following way the contents of papers on that subject given by himself, Menzies and Copland in January 1944:

> . . . pressure on prices from a high level of aggregate demand and a money supply expanded by wartime financial methods; pressure on international reserves from expenditure on imports beyond the

capacity of our exports to finance; *the problems of labour discipline and restraint in wage demands when the bargaining power of labour was to be continually strengthened by the disappearance of the threat of unemployment. . .*[3]

If this emphasis on labour force discipline and inflation was pervasive before the end of the War, it was sharpened in the immediate post-war years by a trade union offensive in which the strength and level of organization of key elements of the working class was amply demonstrated. As Crisp makes clear, the fear of runaway inflation became one of Chifley's major preoccupations and underscored his continuous resistance to wage campaigns by the unions.

The quite obvious antidote to labour force indiscipline arising out of labour shortage was to increase the labour supply by immigration, but there were substantial obstacles to doing so, particularly as it became obvious that there was no prospect of Britain supplying the requisite numbers. So widespread, in fact, was this opposition to immigration that it is possible to see the original immigration programme as a result of élite (as opposed to popular) consensus to just the same extent as multiculturalism was thirty years later.

As one might expect, the populist right of the political spectrum was in the vanguard of opposition to all but British migration with Bolton, the New South Wales president of the Returned Services League, demanding a Royal Commission on the issue and announcing that

> This is a business that should make every Australian hold his breath, not only with indignation but with the fear of what will eventually become . . . Australia being swamped by people of alien thought and dubious loyalty.[4]

On less racist grounds, the fear was widespread that large migration flows would add further stress to the housing crisis. In 1946, a furore erupted over the publication by the Immigration Department of an information booklet for prospective immigrants entitled 'Australia and Your Future' which claimed that houses were available for only 22 shillings per week in the major cities.[5] For this Calwell was bitterly attacked in Parliament by Enid Lyons and widely castigated editorially, even in the pro-immigration press.

A further source of resentment was the conviction that many prospective migrants, particularly 'Balts', were ex-fascists. This suspicion was often linked with the conviction that all migrants (but fascists more so than others) were being imported to Australia for the sole purpose of attacking the pay and conditions of the working class. Throughout the trade union movement, reaction to the immigration programme was bitterly hostile.

From the left-dominated unions in particular, the refrain of opposition to immigration was constant. In 1948 the Federated Iron Workers and South Coast Trades Council fought vigorously against the building of a migrant hostel in Port Kembla, claiming that 'the Balts' who were to occupy it were ex-fascists and that only those who could prove to the Labour Council that they had a clean record should be employed.[6] In the same year the Miners' Federation attempted to ban Poles from underground work declaring that plenty of Australians were willing to work in the pits if owners would only carry out improvements in health and safety conditions which the availability of the Poles provided the opportunity to avoid.[7] Nor was this opposition confined to heavy industry or the left. Unions as non-militant as the Australian Textile Workers added vociferous voices to the exclusionist clamour.

In a situation where large and well-organized groups were vehemently opposed to the immigration programme and where other powerful groups (notably large industrial employers) were equally vehement in its support, the government came to play a key role in the process of ideological production. It had realized early in the piece that the employment issue would be crucial, having been advised by the Commonwealth Immigration Advisory Committee in February, 1946 to

> launch a national publicity campaign conditioning the Australian citizen for the arrival of migrants assuring him that the new citizen will MAKE jobs, not TAKE them.[8]

This advice was taken to heart by the government. Calwell repeatedly assured the nation that

> migrants would not be used to worsen working conditions nor would they be 'used' in any industrial trouble in the industries in which they were employed.[9]

The stand adapted on housing ran parallel. In response to resolutions by all state RSL branches that Australian ex-servicemen should be given priority in housing over 'all immigrant and alien refugees', Calwell stated in February 1947 that 'any newcomer no matter from what country would not be allowed to compete with Australians' for available housing.[10]

Sometimes this hammering out of the idea that migrants would fill gaps rather than contest space already occupied by Australian workers had vaguely comic overtones. In January 1948, for example, Calwell announced that 856 migrants due to arrive aboard the SS General Stewart would not just pick fruit but would 'save' the South Australian and Victorian dried fruit industry.[11] At other times, when more than rhetoric was needed, action was taken to ensure that migrant workers would be prevented from competing for jobs. In the case of the Port Kembla dispute mentioned above, Calwell was able to placate the Federated Ironworkers' Association by reaching an agreement with BHP described by him in the following terms:

> I am happy to be able to inform your Association that the necessary assurances have been given by the Broken Hill Proprietary Company Limited, which undertakes —

i) not to engage any un-naturalized displaced person for its operating staff, i.e., to undertake work with tools on normal award
classifications;

ii) to employ displaced persons on jobs least attractive to
Australian workers and to take advantage of the availability of
displaced persons to effect desired transfers of Australian workers
wherever possible and to give them the benefit of 'pickings'
wherever practicable.[12]

Later that year Calwell intervened in a similar manner in the mines,
implicitly endorsing the segregation of immigrants into lower-paid
surface jobs, and throughout this period he hammered the theme of
migrants filling the jobs that Australians did not want. One of the
best examples was the claim in 1949 that 'one in ten new Australians
working in Australia is engaged in nursing or other domestic work in
hospitals or similar institutions'.[13] It may be assumed that one
reason that 'old' Australians did not compete in this area was that the
award rate for a nurse in 1947 was £2.12.6 per week as compared, for
example, to the rate of £4.0.0. for a cook.

Ideological production did not stop here, however. A sustained
campaign was mounted to assure the public of the essential similar-
ity of 'Europeans'. In advocating the adoption of the term 'New Australian', Calwell stressed that 'the men are handsome and the women
beautiful'.[14] But if Europeans were essentially 'self' then someone
else was essentially 'other': and it was the vigorous reinforcement of
the White Australia Policy which was the equal and opposite reaction to the creation of the 'New Australian'. Nowhere can this better
be seen than in the public utterances of leading politicians. Thus
Chifley in a 1949 radio broadcast:

one of the earliest national ideals of Australia was the establishment of a nation of high living standards with equal opportunity
for all. Early Commonwealth legislators saw that the greatest
possible threat to such an ideal was a pool of cheap labour.

It was then, and still is, a fact that the most likely sources of
cheap labour for those who wished to exploit it were the Asian
countries so near to Australia.[15]

The self/other opposition is just as succinctly put in the statement of
A. G. Beazly, a cabinet minister, that,

Australia will seek migrants of our own kind who could be readily
assimilated and who believe in the standards of living we have
struggled to achieve.

The bogus distinction between European and Asian migrants (the
former making jobs, 'believing' in high living standards the latter, the
reverse), could be maintained because prejudice against Asians was
already deeply ingrained in the vast majority of Australians.
Certainly the post-war government did not invent the exclusion
policy and the impossibility of large-scale non-European immigra-

tion in the late 1940s can be judged from opinion even at the liberal end of the spectrum. For example, in his address to the Australian Institute of Political Science in 1946, Professor Elkins recommended immigration quotas for non-Europeans in order that Australia should not 'be seen to exclude a whole race because of its colour'. He thought an annual quota of fifty would be appropriate for the purpose. (In this Elkins was more liberal than Bertrand Russell who told the Australian Institute of International Affairs in 1950 that 'Asian peoples' should continue to be excluded until they were 'raised to higher social and economic levels', by which time he thought they probably would not want to migrate anyway).

It is, however, important to realize that the administration of the Immigration Restriction Act in the period after the War was carried out with a ferocity which probably exceeded the prejudice of the community as a whole and which, in any case, had the effect of continuously legitimizing and reinforcing those prejudices. For example, in 1948 the *Sydney Morning Herald* editorialized on the 'illiberal and inflexible rulings' which were 'bringing discredit on the White Australia Policy and making enemies in the East'. The two rulings in question were the attempts to deport the Tongan wife of an Australian citizen and to deny entry to the Maori wife of another. In spite of such criticisms the government remained adamant, Calwell remarking as he ordered the deportation of another non-European wife of an Australian citizen in 1949 that 'if the White Australia Policy is to be enforced there must be no exceptions'.[16]

That this was an unnecessary level of zeal is illustrated not only by public criticism and the overturning of some of these decisions in the courts, but also by the refusal to admit even tiny numbers of Asians to fill roles that the public at large would have tolerated on the basis of tradition. A classic vignette is provided by the request of the Graziers Federal Council to recruit a number of Chinese as station cooks to which the response of the Immigration Department was that they could make do with Italians.[17]

It can be seen, then, that two paradoxes were at the heart of the post-war immigration programme, at least at the level of public discourse. These were that an inflow of people which was to transform this country into one of the world's most ethnically diverse was conducted under an ideological umbrella which stressed a continuing homogeneity, the desired product of racial exclusion and enforced assimilation; and that over a period when Australia, on any social or economic indicator, moved rapidly away from Britain, this homogeneity was defined largely in terms of its British origins. In other words, for over half of the post-war period the dominant ideology in both its exclusionist and assimilationist facets was a racist celebration of the superiority of British culture and institutions.

We have attempted to explain the assimilation/exclusion cocktail as (in part) an ideological response to a structural contradiction: the need for mass multi-ethnic migration to service expanding labour-intensive industry in a country where traditional cultural norms and practices, at a number of levels, ensured widespread popular opposition to such immigration. Having established its origins, we must now examine why it was dismembered.

The decline of overt racism

In the mid-1960s, the White Australia Policy was officially abandoned by both major political parties and assimilation was effectively abandoned also, at least in name. On the face of it, this might seem to represent a substantial departure from the past. Radically exclusionist policies had been observed for over eighty years with more or less severity, and they had formed an essential ingredient of the dominant national self concept. Abandoning these practices might seem to indicate fundamental changes in Australian society; but on closer examination the reality is far from impressive.

On 4 August 1965 *The Australian* editorialized as follows:

There are several encouraging omens for the Labor Party in its removal of the term 'White Australia' from its immigration policy. One of the most important is its demonstration that its Dunstans, Whitlams and other younger men are being allowed to play a part in formulating and reforming party policy. Another welcome sign is in the fact that the change comes after an interchange of visits and, presumably, ideas between ALP leaders and the young socialist Prime Minister of Singapore, Mr. Lee Kuan Yew. If there is any connection, we must point out that the motion passed by the conference to change ALP policy does not make it clear whether a Labor government would allow Asian immigration any more than the present one does.

Some of the reported remarks made by the conference delegates seem to indicate that it would not.

Our neighbours in Asia, and particularly in Papua-New Guinea, may be forgiven therefore, if they are not sure if this change is really a reform or just an exercise in wordsmanship.

But we cannot complain too much. White Australia was an offensive and insulting phrase and we must be grateful it has disappeared at last from Australian politics.

This was, in fact, a fair summary of what had actually happened, and not just within the ALP. The debates on policy changes in Parliament were characterized by a high level of bipartisan agreement about the desirable limits of policy reform and these limits were set fairly close to existing practice. Essentially, people of non-European origin would be permitted to enter Australia but on the basis of much stricter entry criteria than Europeans; and the numbers permitted to enter would be restricted so as to preserve the 'homogeneity' of the population. Opperman, the Minister of Immigration, summed up the new policy as follows:

No annual quota is contemplated. The numbers of people entering — though limited relative to our total population — will be somewhat greater than, but will be controlled by careful assessment of the individuals' qualifications and the basic aim of preserving a homogeneous population will be maintained. The changes are of course, not intended to meet general labour shortages or to permit the large-scale admission of workers from Asia.[18]

Sir Keith Wilson, a prominent Liberal member, stated bluntly that the policy changes were both bipartisan and unlikely to make much difference to anything since preference would continue to be given to Northern Europeans characterized by

. . . their high standard of living and ability to learn English within five years . . . while . . . southern Europeans and numbers from other countries . . . (would) . . . vary according to the test to which I have referred[19]

Essentially, then, the new policy permitted the entry of small groups of middle-class non-Europeans, their numbers controlled so as to render them socially invisible and those numbers always subject to the availability of preferred immigrant groups.

The change from the doctrine of assimilation to that of integration was to be of equally limited significance. The minister who presided over this change of policy, Billy Snedden, was of the conviction that:

Australia has no history of social pluralism . . . it may develop gradually and to a limited extent but that is not something to be forced on any nation or any people, including Australians. That would not be social pluralism but social masochism . . . no nation in history has set out to develop a multi-racial society.[20]

What was involved, in fact, was the recognition that the nature of the migration process itself implied that the first generation might find complete assimilation impossible and that some of the difficulties experienced by them might best be alleviated by working through the now-legitimate 'national group'. The basic goal remained the same, however, and that goal was eventual complete assimilation to an 'Australian' mainstream culture. As Snedden put it: 'We ask particularly of migrants that they be substantially Australians in the first generation and completely Australians in the second generation.'[21]

In other words, a degree of cultural pluralism was accepted as an inevitable consequence of the migration programme, but, although the road might be more circuitous than had previously been thought, the cultural goal was exactly that of the late 1940s.

In reality both the modification of the rules of racial exclusion and the toning down of assimilation were minimal responses to circumstances over which the government had little control. As such they are indicative of only minor changes in the attitudes of the political elite towards questions of race, ethnicity and national identity. Still less were they likely to represent (or cause) changes in wider public attitudes.

The major reason for both changes lay in Australia's shifting industrial structure and international economic position. Throughout the 1950s and early 1960s the importance of Japan and South-East Asia as trading partners increased rapidly. For obvious reasons, the White Australia Policy in its crude form was an embarrassment in this process. This embarrassment increased markedly in the early 1960s with the achievement of independence by several former colonies whose leaders were more likely (and more able) to exert pressure over racist exclusionism. This, it will be noted, was not a process affecting Australia alone. In 1965 the United States which had, over the previous twenty years, similarly become involved in the expanding Pacific economy, also reformed its immigration laws, abolishing national quotas and replacing them with regulations similar to Australia's. In both the Australian and American context one might describe these changes as retaining an essentially exclusionist and discriminatory immigration policy, while minimizing both the appearance of discrimination and the effect of that discrimination on those most able to be heard when complaining: the skilled, educated and internationally mobile artificers of an increasingly integrated international economy.

International factors also precipitated the move away from assimilation. By the mid-1960s the supply of European refugees had long since dried up and the gap in living standards between Australia and Europe was fast closing. Not only did this make Australia a less attractive destination, but other destinations were appearing much more attractive to migrants from Australia's traditional source countries.

By the mid-1960s high rates of growth in Northern Europe meant that new migrants from preferred source countries were becoming harder to find, and that substantial re-migration from Australia was taking place, particularly by people from preferred ethnic groups such as the Dutch and Germans. In addition, the nature of arrivals from source countries was changing rapidly in the direction of people less obviously assimilable. By 1965 most Italian immigration was of unskilled people of Southern peasant background, in marked contrast to the overall trend in the 1950s. In 1968 the Turkish immigration agreement was signed, permitting the immigration of the first group of people of largely Islamic background.

None of this went unnoticed in an Australia whose appetite for continued immigration of industrial workers was as voracious as ever. At Citizenship Conventions from the late 1950s concern was expressed constantly on this issue by both industrialists and bureaucrats. This concern mounted over the 1960s to the extent that by 1967 the government was prepared to accede, in the Turkish immigration agreement, to a range of conditions such as job and accommodation guarantees which it had flatly refused in negotiating the renewal of the Italian immigration agreement seven years earlier. Integration was essentially a public admission that migrants would continue to have specific welfare needs beyond the immediate post-arrival period and that what was increasingly referred to as the 'national group' might be of assistance as a vehicle in providing this.

If the major propelling forces in the two policy changes were to be found in international relations, there were domestic causes also. The increasing militancy of Aboriginal groups and organizations, as well as the increasing international stigma of Australia's system of virtual apartheid, resulted in the referendum of 1967, which for the first time granted citizenship to Aboriginal people. Aboriginal protests, such as the 'freedom rides', modelled on actions of the United States Civil Rights Movement, made it difficult to sustain the myth of a 'homogeneous white society'. Sometimes Aboriginal activists linked their struggle with opposition to racist immigration laws. In the Nancy Prassad case, which gained considerable publicity, a six-year old Fijian girl was snatched away from the police at Sydney Airport as she was about to be deported. The snatcher was Charles Perkins, who later led the Freedom Rides, and is today Head of the Department of Aboriginal Affairs. Such developments made overt racism hard to sustain.

As an overt policy, assimilation also had lost its original rationale by the late 1960s. If our previous analysis is correct and assimilation was essentially an ideological construct facilitating the acceptance of the immigration programme by a largely xenophobic population, then this ideology had been so successful it was no longer needed. Largely due to the extraordinary prosperity of the 1950s and 1960s migrants were absorbed into the labour force without major disruption, except in the recessions of 1952 and 1961. This labour force quickly developed the characteristic segmentation detailed in Chapter Two, and this was widely touted as a benefit to the 'Australian' worker. For example, in a Citizenship Convention address of 1958 Arthur Monk, Secretary of the ACTU, stated that:

> the introduction of the migrant worker at the bottom of the ladder often meant promotion or upgrading for Australian workers and relieved them of the necessity to seek employment in remote areas or of an arduous character.

In such circumstances, it was difficult to sustain opposition to immigration since the everyday experience of Australian-born workers was simply not one of having to compete in any direct or general sense with migrants. In the mid-1960s mass immigration was a fact of almost two decades standing, as was prosperity. Immigration would not be seriously contested while prosperity lasted.

Given the limited nature of the real changes made, the factors detailed above ensured that the retreat from assimilation and White Australia policies took place with little controversy. That any retreat at all took place from the habits of mind which underlay them is more questionable, however, and this is largely because the discourse of the mid-1960s had not been couched in terms which required a re-appraisal of these habits of mind. The superiority of 'British'-derived cultural practice was still covertly asserted in integrationist policies, and the essential distinction between 'European' and 'Asian' preserved in a double-barrelled immigration policy. Instructive in this respect were the debates on the Turkish immigration agreement. Throughout the debate, racist stereotypes were thick in the air. For example, Clyde Cameron (who was minister responsible for im-migration as recently as 1974-5) was at pains to reassure honourable members that the Turks are not 'a dark-skinned people who have nothing in common with the Australian people'.[22] He also recom-mended setting up immigration offices in Ljubljana and Zagreb on the grounds that Croats and Slovenians are 'more suitable to the Australian way of life than Serbs who live around Belgrade.'

Notes

1. Chapters 3 and 4 draw heavily on A. Jakubowicz, M. Morrissey, and J. Palser, *Ethnicity, Class and Social Policy in Australia*, SWRC Report No.46, University of NSW: Social Welfare Research Centre May 1984.
2. J. I. Martin, *The Migrant Presence*, Sydney: George Allen & Unwin 1978, p.23.
3. H. E. Coombs, *Trial Balance*, Melbourne: Macmillan 1981, p.49. Our emphasis.
4. *Sydney Morning Herald*, 24 July 1947.
5. e.g. *Sydney Morning Herald*, 31 July 1947.
6. *Sydney Morning Herald*, 26 March 1948.
7. *Sydney Morning Herald*, 24 September 1948.
8. Commonwealth Immigration Advisory Council Report, Canberra 1946, p.36.
9. *Sydney Morning Herald*, 7 April 1948.
10. *Sydney Morning Herald*, 2 April 1947.
11. *Sydney Morning Herald*, 17 January 1948.
12. A. Calwell, to E. Thornton quoted in: A.Markus 'Labour and immigration', Postwar Reconstruction Seminar Canberra: ANU 1982.
13. Calwell in *Hansard*, House of Representatives, 8 September 1949, pp.39-44.
14. *Sydney Morning Herald*, 16 December 1947.
15. B. Chifley, 'Australia's Immigration Policy', *Current Notes* 20:5 April, 1949.
16. *Sydney Morning Herald*, 12 July 1949.
17. *Sydney Morning Herald*, 2 July 1948.

18.   Jakubowicz, Morrissey and Palser, p.40.
19.   Sir Keith Wilson, *Hansard*, 24 August 1966, p.275.
20.   Jakubowicz, Morrissey and Palser, p.40.
21.   *Ibid.*
22.   C. Cameron, *Hansard*, 15 August 1968, p.224.

4.
The Construction of Ethnicity 1972-1987

The family of the nation

Most people, if asked when Australia made its first steps towards multiculturalism, would nominate the Whitlam period and, equally likely, would mention Whitlam's first Minister for Immigration, Al Grassby, as being the architect of this policy. What actually happened is, however, a rather more complex story. We would argue, in fact, that, far from developing a fully-articulated ideology of state-sponsored cultural pluralism, the Whitlam Government merely provided the preconditions for the emergence of such an ideology; and that, furthermore, the full articulation of this ideology by the Fraser Government was a key strategy in a conservative restructuring of the welfare state whose main purpose was the demolition of Whitlam-style social democracy. In all of this the changing nature of politics and Australian society, itself largely responsive to a rapidly-developing international economy, provides the essential context of explanation. Before proceeding to an analysis of these processes, however, it is important to demonstrate that the Whitlam Government did not come to power with the intention of proselytizing cultural pluralism. The lingering impression that it did so is the effect of distorted historical hindsight.

We might begin by examining the central question of immigration policies. As we have argued in the previous chapter, the abandonment of the White Australia Policy in the mid-1960s caused very little concern for the simple reason that it was not anticipated that the new, supposedly 'non-discriminatory' policy would make much difference to the actual composition of the immigrant intake. The experience of the later 1960s did nothing to dispel this belief, which extended as far as the liberal intelligentsia. For example, in a compendium of essays around the theme of racism published in 1971, A. C. Palfreeman concluded, after examining 'the arithmetic':

> On the basis of these figures, it is likely that some 4,000 non-Europeans will acquire permanent residence in 1971 and that the

annual rate will increase over the next few years. But even at this
rate it will be a long time before the proportion of non-Europeans
in the population reaches the figure it was in 1901.[1]
Given that Palfreeman calculated the 1901 figure at 1.25 per cent of
the population, it can be seen that the anticipated change was very
small indeed.

During the Whitlam period it was freely claimed that Australia's
immigration policy no longer discriminated on grounds of race: yet
the reality was greatly different from the rhetoric as much stricter
criteria continued to be applied to non-European applicants
compared to Europeans in a systematic effort to ensure that non-
European immigration was restricted in number and class background. In fact, the government was extremely sensitive to charges
that it would permit the 'Asianization' of Australia. As one ALP
member put it, in response to such an accusation,

to suggest that . . . (a non-discriminatory immigration policy)
. . . indicates an open door to Asiatic migration or the breakdown
of the Australian way of life is malicious in the extreme.[2]

Caution on this topic can be seen behind Grassby's frequent advocacy of what he termed 'chain migration' as opposed to 'mass
migration', the hidden agenda being, of course that to tie eligibility
closely to the question of pre-existing family networks in Australia
was at this time to impose *de facto* an extreme restriction on non-
European immigration, given the tiny size of the non-European
population. In fact the logic of this procedure was carried one step
forward by Grassby's successor, Cameron, who informed the Parliament late in 1974 that his department was in the process of preparing
a set of 'national quotas' as the basis for future immigration policy.[3]

We have previously identified an emphasis on the supposed incompatibility of non-European immigration and the 'Australian way
of life' as a key component of national identity. Whilst not affirming
or proselytizing such a view (except when backed into a corner), the
Whitlam Government did very little to contest it, preferring instead
to sweep the unpalatable fact that immigration policies remained
highly discriminatory under a carpet of rhetoric about non-
discrimination. In this they probably had very little choice if their
actions are seen in the context of the electorate or of the fact that a
substantial fraction of the party's old guard (most notably Fred
Daly, the Leader of the House) continued to view with suspicion
even the heavily restricted numbers of non-Europeans then being
granted entry. The fact remains, however, that at the level of public
debate the idea that the maintenance of a uniquely Australian
character and way of life was contingent upon a degree of racist exclusionism was never really challenged and was, in fact, affirmed in
practice.

This disjuncture between rhetoric and practice was replicated to
an extent in the development of multiculturalism. The term 'multi-

cultural' does not appear in the *Hansard* index until 8 March 1977, almost 18 months into the Fraser ministry, which seems to be a fairly poignant comment on the degree of priority accorded it by the Whitlam ministry. Yet four years before that date Grassby had delivered to a symposium a speech entitled *A Multicultural Society for the Future* which Jean Martin saw as 'a manifesto for the plural society which . . . he was to acknowledge and promote'.[4] As what has come to be known as the 'Family of the Nation' speech has been accorded considerable importance in the development of multi-culturalism, it is appropriate to examine it closely.

The most important point about the speech is that it does, indeed, make an explicit rejection of assimilationism:

> the increasing diversity of Australia society has . . . rendered untenable any prospects there might have been twenty years ago of fully assimilating newcomers to the Australian way of life, to use a phrase common at the time.[5]

Apart from this unequivocal declaration, however, the rest of the speech is extremely vague and as much concerned with issues of equity and participation as with the question of cultural pluralism. Apart from a demand that school curricula should be made 'cultur-ally relevant', the main references in a section on policy changes are to the structural and economic marginalization of migrants and the speech is consistently vague too about the distinction between prescription and description. Reading it gives no clear idea whether we are being asked simply to accept that 'ethnic communities exist and refuse to be assimilated', or whether this pluralism should be in-stitutionalized. Still less does it have to say on the limits of pluralism or what form its institutionalization might take.

Even given the limitations of the speech as a 'manifesto', there must also be some doubt about who Grassby was speaking for, other than himself, particularly within the state apparatus. Certainly, bureaucratic opposition to any idea of pluralism was enormous and in any case, less than a year after the delivery of the speech, Grassby was out of Parliament, the Department had been split up and the major responsibility for matters affecting migrants was vested in Clyde Cameron, to whose disdainful views on cultural pluralism we have already referred.

In summary, then, the production or maintenance of a 'multi-cultural' society was a project to which the Whitlam Government attached little or no importance at a *legislative* level, and the major public description of multiculturalism was, in reality, a highly am-bivalent document, and one whose generality of acceptance within the government was at best questionable. Yet within five years of the 'Family of the Nation' speech, a full-blown 'ism' with bipartisan acceptance had emerged, and had been given material expression in the Galbally Report. The obvious question arising is why multiculturalism made the transition from the wings of public discourse to centre stage in so short a time.

We have already shown that one of the major causes of the abandonment of assimilation was anxiety about the availability of sufficient migrants to power the economic boom of the 1960s. By 1972 this anxiety had largely vanished as the boom halted. In fact, the Whitlam Government quickly *reduced* the migrant intake upon winning office. Nevertheless, the doctrine of integration had important consequences in that it legitimated for the first time the entry of groups organized around a common ethnicity into the political arena, and also gave a degree of credence to the proposition that certain types of social services might be delivered effectively through the medium of ethnic organizations, a view supported by a number of prominent academics.

Simultaneous with this process was the emergence, as a result of a number of official and academic enquiries, of a perception of migrants as being a relatively disadvantaged and marginalized group of people.

At first these two pressures produced only small results, but towards the end of the 1960s changes became evident. Thus the Italian welfare organization Co.As.It. was formed in 1967 and the Australian Greek Welfare Society in 1969, with the principal activists being drawn largely from well-established professionals or business people. Over the next few years a network of welfare-oriented organizations was gradually formed, most of it on a voluntary basis and with very little state support.

By the time the Whitlam Government came to power, the ALP had adopted as part of its official policy the notion that migrants were a disadvantaged group requiring special attention and in the 1972 election campaign Labor politicians energetically courted what was increasingly being labelled as the 'migrant vote'. In short, both the political consciousness and the organizations requisite to the development of a political process revolving around questions of ethnicity were present in more than embryonic form.

The 1972 Labor Government was one which saw itself as having a generalized reforming mission. The existence of disadvantaged groups — such as migrants — even after over twenty years of general prosperity was seen as clear evidence that conservative strategies of distributing welfare entirely through the labour market were deeply flawed and resulted in considerable inequalities of opportunity. A more interventionist strategy was needed. In relation to the specific question of migrants, the thrust of this policy can be seen from Whitlam's speech to the 1970 Citizenship Convention which we quote at some length below. It will be noted that the main thrust of the speech is in terms of the structural disadvantage of migrants. Concerns about community relations and cultural pluralism are notable by their absence.

The fact is that for too long most Australians have assumed that the benefit of migration is all on one side. We tend to assume that mere permission to settle among us is a boon of such transcendental quality that simple gratitude and silent compliance are the sole duties of those upon whom this benefit is conferred. We have never been prepared to treat urgently, for reasons either of justice or expediency, the matter of trade and professional qualifications. We have thought it natural that migrants should be content to fill the lowest paid occupations, accept the costliest housing in the ugliest areas, send their children to the most crowded and least equipped schools, and accept worse health services, worse public transport, fewer recreational amenities and poorer urban services than are available in many European cities and centres from which they have come.

Australians now have to realize that in matters of health, housing, education, social welfare and urban services, Australia compares increasingly unfavorably with the very countries which provide — and must continue to provide — most of our migrants. We should no longer expect migrants to settle for the second rate, particularly when so much of what passes for our best is itself second rate by the standards of the countries with which we compare ourselves.

(Migrants) have not the social capital for their establishment in marriage and accommodation. One migrant in every twelve becomes a victim of mental illness. Last year 213,500 migrants left Australia and took up residence elsewhere, mostly for housing reasons, but often because of health costs.[6]

The two main areas in which the Labor Government was to take action were those of social welfare and education, the former being the more important in terms of the development of multiculturalism. Within this area the programme that Martin describes as:

having the most potential for change in relation to migrant questions was the Australian Assistance Plan which provided the vehicle by which the scattered groups of migrant and migrant-oriented welfare organizations could move towards the centres of political power and also acted as a catalyst to the development of more integrated and articulate migrant organizations.[7]

This was not because of the contents of the Plan itself, which had very little to say about migrants *directly*; rather, it was an indirect result of the fact that the Australian Assistance Plan (AAP), and, indeed, the whole strand of Labor welfare philosophy it represented, was highly suited to accommodate and nourish the aspirations of the developing ethnic welfare lobby. The Labor perception that Menzian free market welfare allocation had, in fact, marginalized whole groups of people led naturally to the idea of whole groups of people

— migrants being one such group — becoming the 'targets' for particular social welfare programmes. From here, given the ALP's suspicion of a Commonwealth bureaucracy widely believed to be prone to partiality against Labor, and also given the populist element in the party's general philosophy, it became only a short step to construing these marginalized groups as 'communities' whose participation in the political process was to be encouraged and whose internal solidarity was to be promoted through a process of 'community development'.

Essentially, the aim of the AAP was to provide an integrated system of welfare services with high levels of grassroots participation, but within the context of a national framework. The primary vehicle for implementing the plan was a series of Regional Councils of Social Development, most of which had committees concerned with migrant issues and which were described by Martin as having

> had an unprecedented import because they were part of a national authority and plugged into a system with the capacity for nation-wide communication and because they had the concrete task of developing ways of dealing with migrant welfare problems and engaging migrants in community development.[8]

The most obvious concrete development to emerge from the AAP was the formation of the Ethnic Communities Councils of South Australia and Victoria (in 1974) and of New South Wales (in 1975), but probably its most significant effects were less tangible: the contribution made by the operation of the AAP to the metamorphosis of ethnic groups into ethnic 'communities' with 'leaders' was more important than anything else it achieved, at least in the context of our present concerns.

In a society divided by socio-economic inequalities the notion of community is always problematic, as we shall argue later; but before doing so it is necessary to look at some other pressures which were tending in the same direction as those operating within the AAP, also within the area of social welfare.

In early 1973 Grassby began to set up a series of Migrant Task Forces with wide-ranging review functions. It was a sign of the times that the first of these, set up in New South Wales under the chairmanship of a Labor MHR, was immediately and bitterly attacked for its lack of any migrant members. This was quickly remedied and thereafter the Task Forces were expanded to include a number of migrant activists, some of whom were later to be prominent in the development of multiculturalism in the Fraser period. For example, prominent on the Victorian Task Force was Walter Lippman, who had already served on a number of other bodies, including the Immigration Advisory Council and who, in 1971, had petitioned the Australian Institute of Political Science Conference on Migration in the following terms:

In the last ten years we have gingerly shifted the accent from migrant assimilation to migrant integration, recognizing that there are differences in cultural background, experience, environment and outlook which distinguish most migrants and even their children from the majority of Australians.

For most migrants ethnic background is meaningful because it is an important part of their personality. Coming to a strange country, they find security and a sense of belonging in their own national or ethnic group. We are doing ourselves a great disservice in not openly recognizing them and utilizing them for development of a multicultural society. Let us do away with ambivalence: acculturation is taking place among the immigrants but we must not cripple their personalities by expecting them to renounce part of themselves.[9]

Perhaps because of the participation of 'community' leaders of this sort and also, perhaps, due to the proximity of the Task Forces to Grassby, the reports produced by them are closest in tone to what later emerged as multiculturalism as anything produced under the aegis of the Whitlam Government. In general, the reports covered a wide range of socio-economic, legal and cultural issues and usually took a line heavily in favour of community development, stressing the ethnic group in service delivery. One commentator in fact has stated that a considerable amount of the groundwork for the Galbally Report is to be found in the Task Force reports, and another sign of things to come was the recommendation from one report in 1974 'that a national workshop be held to explore the concept and implications of the "Family of the Nation" '.

Most of this activity had little *immediate* material result at any other level than the production of printed pages, but one extremely important outcome was the rapid expansion of the system of government-financed community welfare workers, of whom 49 were in employment by the end of 1974. This represented a degree of professionalization (and consequently enhanced opportunities for access and networking) of a group of previously volunteer activists to whom Martin referred as 'a new body of definers'[10] of the ethnic dimension, and it was also to be a development carried forward in subsequent years.

The federal election of 1974, which saw Grassby lose his seat, the deepening economic crisis, with attendant austerity measures, as well as the government's decision to disband the Immigration Department, all meant that 1974 was a temporary high water mark in the encroachment of multiculturalism into the domain of public discussion and practice. It still represented a fairly inchoate set of notions and was a clearly accepted principle only in scattered parts of the state apparatus. It was to be left to the Fraser Government to synthesize these fragments into what we have previously described as

a fully-fledged 'ism'. At the level of practice, however, the limited initiatives already taken had revealed some very problematic features
in what we may (perhaps somewhat flippantly) call national family
formation.

We have argued that the Whitlam years were crucial in the legitimation of two linked concepts: that of migrants as constituency and
that of ethnic group as community. As J. Zubrzycki, Professor of
Sociology at the Australian National University, was later to put it:

> What we believe Australia should be working towards is not a one-
> ness, but a unity, not a similarity, but a composite, not a melting
> pot but a voluntary bond of dissimilar people sharing a common
> political and institutional structure. (Multiculturalism means) . . .
> that the spokesmen (sic) for every culture should be heard, that
> they should have a chance to put their case in the community
> debate, that they should be taken seriously in high places. Among
> the groups that are 'in' (e.g. trade unions, employees, the estab-
> lished churches, the AMA) this dialogue goes on all the time . . .
> *Multiculturalism means ethnic communities getting into the act.*[11]

What this means is that the ethnic middle class should be empowered
and accorded the same access and status as other élite groups: that
society works by renegotiation and compromise between entrenched
sectional interests, of which ethnic 'communities' form a sub-group;
and that the credentials of the ethnic middle class for entrance to the
players' enclosure is the existence, and their leadership of, ethnic
'communities'. The unanswered questions all revolve around the
problematic notion of community. Quite apart from the self-evident
fact that the interests of a steelworker made redundant by accelerating structural change may be very different from those of a
comfortably-ensconced professor of the same ethnicity, there are
also severe problems about accommodating to this vision the existence of communities which cut across ethnicities. Martin, for example, details the confusions which arose in the operation of the
Regional Councils about whether migrant representatives were there
to represent an ethnicity or a locality and also points out the extreme
differences in the level of 'community development' (meaning socio-
economic mobility?) between ethnic groups in a situation where
there is competition for scarce resources.

In the context of what we shall refer to as conservative multiculturalism there is, in short, an implicit social theory, summed up by
two social commentators (in the period when the aforesaid conservative multiculturalism had reached the zenith of its influence) as
follows:

> Australian society is built on the basis of individuals and groups
> trying to maximize their interests;
>   . . . essentially, it is a free market society — in which in-
> dividuals and groups bargain and negotiate for their economic
> and social interests . . .

> . . . the role of Government is to provide opportunities for individuals and groups to commence such bargaining on a roughly equal footing; i.e., all that is required is to provide opportunities for people to get to a position where they can 'compete' for resources and services . . .
>
> . . .consequently the 'well-being' of migrants is defined in terms of access to Government services. It is not defined in terms of attempting to change structures or in terms of providing better/more income security; better jobs; high status work; or in terms of *equity* in resource allocation;
>
> in essence this is a *status quo* view of society; the Report does not want structures/institutions to change; it does not want any major changes to power structures or decision making processes; rather, it wants to incorporate the 'new ethnics' into the existing game but only after the rules have been established, and the umpires decided upon.[12]

During the Whitlam years this view of society had been, to an extent, contested at the level of government. In the period 1975 to 1983 it was to become both dominant and explicit.

Neo-conservatism and multiculturalism

The Fraser Government which came to power in November 1975 had as its objective the dismantling of the structures resulting from the initiatives of the Whitlam years. Incensed by the decline in the profit-wage ratio resulting from the wages boom of the early 1970s, obsessed by budget deficits as a result of the spreading orthodoxy of Friedmanite economics, their individualist social philosophy affronted by the ALP's tentative move away from residualist social policies, the conservative parties proceeded to abolish the AAP, Medibank and a range of lesser programmes with as much haste as political expediency permitted. In many ways it was back to the late 1960s with a vengeance sharpened by the now obviously final collapse of the long boom. There were, however, two major exceptions. As we have seen, the pre-1972 policy of the Coalition with regard to migrants rested unequivocally on the need for a population which was culturally and, to a large extent, 'racially' homogeneous: even the official abandonment of complete assimilation of the first generation as a policy goal had not opened the door an inch to any notion of continuing cultural pluralism in subsequent generations. The abandonment of the White Australia Policy had been largely a carefully-controlled exercise in international public relations. Yet it was to be the Fraser Government which loudly espoused the ideology of cultural pluralism and which also became the first twentieth-century Australian government to permit large-scale immigration from Asia. The old ideologies of nationalism based on common race, culture and ancestry, problematic at any time, became totally untenable as a result of these actions.

As we shall see, the admission of South-East Asian refugees was forced on the government by circumstances largely outside its control, but no such overt pressure for the advent of multiculturalism was exerted. There were no mass campaigns demanding the various provisions of the Galbally Report, yet a government that was prepared to tough out a general strike over the abolition of Medibank was prepared to indulge in new forms of expenditure on multicultural programmes. We shall argue that the Galbally programme was virtually self-financing and designed not to meet a mass demand, but to achieve a limited political goal: the incorporation into conservative politics of the ethnic middle classes. The Galbally programme had many aspects but its *essential* purpose was to trade cultural radicalism for political conservatism and in so doing to assure the people in question that Zubrzycki's demand had been met and that the 'leaders' of ethnic communities were, indeed, being 'taken seriously' in high places.

In this sense both the espousal of a national identity based on cultural pluralism and, as we shall argue, the decision to permit South-East Asian immigration, were products of an élite consensus rather than responses to widespread changes in the beliefs and attitudes of the population as a whole. In a very real sense, the problematic nature of multiculturalism derives from its origins and the economic context in which it has operated. Multiculturalism has ensured a sharp increase in the achievable status and cultural acceptance of the ethnic *middle* classes but, since its inception as government policy, has operated over a decade in which the life chances of the ethnic *working* class have been ravaged by unemployment, falling living standards and an accelerating urban crisis in which yesterday's cheap migrant suburbs are becoming rookeries for the middle class and the socially mobile.

The conservatives' conversion to the multicultural cause began soon after the 1972 election, and was based partly on the perception that the ALP had more successfully captured the ethnic vote and, as the Whitlam ministry progressed, on the observation that the ethnic middle class was becoming increasingly drawn into participation in some of the very programmes that the Opposition was determined to terminate. There was no illusion that migrants had voted ALP in any monolithic way but there was a conviction that if no alternatives were offered to the opportunities for status achievement and access to policy formation currently under construction by Labor, then there was the possibility of producing an image of the Coalition as uncaring and ignorant of migrant issues.

In this the political course of the key ethnic organizations was also a factor. The larger welfare organizations such as Co.As.It. and Australian Greek Welfare Society, as well as the Ethnic Communities

Councils, were constitutionally and studiously non-partisan in party political terms. Complete marginalization of these groups accompanied by deep general welfare cuts, however, might see this situation change and a natural alliance emerge between the ethnic middle class and the ALP. How to prevent this was the basic problem facing the opposition.

The options available to the shadow Minister for Immigration, Malcolm Fraser, and his successor, Michael McKellar, were limited. Whatever their ambiguities (and there were many) the social policy initiatives of the ALP had been loosely based on the premise that Australian society *systematically* and *structurally* disadvantaged whole groups of people and that, if equality of opportunity were to be achieved, then there was need for continuous and extensive state intervention to offset the intrinsic tendency of the system to disadvantage these groups. According to this model, migrants suffered, not because they were migrants but because of what Australian society tended to do to migrants. The answer, as we have seen, was a social policy based on a group approach.

This did not appear to be an option for conservatives since for them it is unacceptable to propose that a 'free market' economy can be characterized by these intrinsic tendencies. At the heart of conservative residualist social policy is the proposition that the only welfare function of the state is to provide a safety net for those individuals who, because of their own pathology, have not succeeded in looking after themselves. The approach of the AAP, through which the ALP was successfully building bridges to the ethnic middle class, was anathema on philosophical grounds even had it not stood condemned by the 'need' for spending cuts and smaller government.

The horns of this philosophical dilemma could, however, be neatly bridged in the case of migrants since in this case it was possible to argue that group disadvantage arose from factors which were not intrinsic to the system: 'national' prejudice, lack of information and lack of main language competence. Moreover these could be combated through a strategy by which the 'community' became a primary vehicle for alleviating the *effects* of disadvantage and also for eliminating some of its *causes* — particularly those of prejudice and lack of cultural understanding.

The most complete articulation of this conservative multiculturalism was the *Review of Post-Arrival Programmes and Services to Migrants* (Galbally Report) which was tabled in Parliament in 1978 and was to be a base point of reference for government policies relating to migrants over much of the following decade. In order to decode this document it is necessary to set it in its wider political context.

The terms of reference of the Galbally committee included the requirement that it took account of five 'recent relevant enquiries', the most important of which was the Task Force on Co-ordination in Welfare and Health (Bailey Committee) which had reported at the end of 1976. Essentially, the Bailey Report had provided a manual for the reinstatement of Liberal residualism in social welfare policies and its inclusion as an item in Galbally's terms of reference indicates clearly that migrants' social welfare would be viewed within this context. In part this was to be achieved by actual spending cuts in programmes from which immigrants had previously benefitted. Thus the Report's conclusion that allowing tax rebates on remittances sent overseas was an 'unreasonable burden' on the Australian taxpayer provided the government with the opportunity to abolish these rebates in the 1978 budget, producing over the next triennium a saving more than 50 per cent greater than the *total* expenditure on Galbally-originated programmes. In addition the emphasis on ethnic groups (now 'communities') as vehicles of service delivery meant that these services would be characterized by a high degree of volunteerism and also that individual groups could be played off against each other in the competition for extremely limited resource allocations.

The other relevant element of the political context from which the Report emerged is that it was not simply the brainchild of the four members of the Committee of Review and their secretariat. As we have pointed out, many of the basic positions of Galbally had been worked out during the Whitlam period. They had remained largely ignored since they were fairly tangential to the main concerns of the government at that time. During the mid-1970s, however, these issues (of community development and support, cultural maintenance, access for community 'leaders') were taken up energetically by McKellar and his staff in an assiduous courtship of the more prominent 'leaders'. In general the message was to be that the conservatives had learned their lesson and were now fully conscious of the legitimacy of ethnic organizations and the validity of their claims.[13]

Initially the campaign was centred around Labor's abolition of the Department of Immigration, but increasingly the restoration of the Department became a means rather than an end and issues of cultural pluralism were pushed to the fore. We have already argued that the stirrings of support for cultural pluralism in the Whitlam Labor Government had been fairly marginal and their implications unclear. Galbally is — on the surface, at least, — unequivocal. Thus we pointed out that the 'Family of the Nation' speech leaves us in the dark as to whether advocacy of multiculturalism is a demand for recognition of what is or for a striving towards what should be. Not so Galbally: multiculturalism is *both* description and prescription.

9.1 We recognize the extensive cultural and racial diversity existing in Australia and we are conscious of the problems and the advantages to the nation such diversity presents.

9.6 We are convinced that migrants have the right to maintain their cultural and racial identity and that it is clearly in the best interests of our nation that they should be encouraged and assisted to do so if they wish. Provided that ethnic identity is not stressed at the expense of society at large, but is interwoven into the fabric of our nationhood by the process of multicultural interaction, then the community as a whole will benefit substantially and its democratic nature will be reinforced. The knowledge that people are identified with their cultural background and ethnic group enables them to take their place in their new society with confidence if their ethnicity has been accepted by the community.[14]

And furthermore

If we are to achieve the real benefits of a multicultural society, its development must be guided, supported and given direction by independent experts of high calibre.

This lack of ambivalence was more apparent than real, however. As has consistently been the case with others, Galbally is less than adequate on the subject of just how cultures are to be preserved. The report gives a startlingly all-embracing definition of culture, and a definition of race no less startling in its dismissiveness.

9.2. Our ethnic groups are distinguishable by various factors. For our purposes we need only identify the two major relevant varying attributes of ethnicity as culture and race.

9.3. It is desirable to define our concept of culture. We believe it is a way of life, that 'complex whole which includes knowledge, belief, art, morals, law, customs, and any other capabilities and habits acquired by man as a member of Society'. (1) The concept of race is clear.

(1) Taylor, *Primitive Culture*, London 1891 (sic)[15]

Soon after, the Report addresses the question of how cultures, thus defined, are to be preserved. (Significantly, it has nothing to say about how to preserve races nor, indeed, about whether or not races should be preserved). After stating that

. . . the most significant and appropriate bodies to be involved in the fostering and preservation of cultures are the ethnic organizations themselves.[16]

It goes on to ask what 'community resources' are required for this task. It answers the question with the following list:

— meeting facilities, books, slides, tapes etc., in municipal libraries:
— bigger funding of 'ethnic' arts by the Australia Council: and
— cultural agreement with other countries.[17]

This hubristic juxtaposition of heroic definitions of culture and Disneyland formulae for their maintenance is only in part the product of intellectual poverty. As we argue in Chapter Seven any attempt to tear apart the questions of culture and socio-economic structure is bound to arrive at a trivial definition of culture. Any compounding of that error by ignoring systematic inequalities which have cultural/ethnic aspects will trivialize all the more thoroughly.

The Galbally report devotes four out of 122 pages of text to questions of employment. The treatment of this subject is cursory with the most significant conclusion being that

> While we believe that the main causes of unemployment among migrants are the same as for Australian-born workers, inadequate English certainly makes things more difficult for migrants in many cases.[18]

The first half of this conclusion was based on the two-page statistical analysis presented in the Report's appendix 57 which disaggregates no further than a comparison of Australian and overseas-born (despite the Report's general insistence on the importance of ethnic communities). As we have shown in Chapter Two such comparisons are virtually meaningless.

The main functions of Galbally, then, were to set up and institutionalize an 'ethnicity model' of disadvantage in which questions of social structure were ignored or mystified; to provide a complex framework of patronage and opportunity for status through a 'community'-based welfare system of Grant-in-Aid workers, ethnic schools, Migrant Resource Centres, etc; and to provide the mechanism for ideological reinforcement of this model by setting up the Australian Institute of Multicultural Affairs (AIMA), a research and policy advice body with Galbally as its first chairperson and Petro Georgiou, formerly one of Fraser's speechwriters, as its first Director. Through the Fraser Ministry this ethnicity model was continually reinforced, most notably by the AIMA review of the Galbally programmes[19], which, in 1982, provided a virtually complete vindication of these. By the end of the Fraser period cultural pluralism had become virtually the exclusive context of discourse on matters relating to immigrants.

The installation of cultural pluralism as a dominant ideology was an extremely profound change in the nature of public discourse in Australia, but in the late 1970s another, equally important, took place. In 1978 10,191 Indochinese refugees were admitted to Australia. In the following years the level of Indochinese entry was increased to give a total of 69,877 by the end of 1981.[20] These were not the sort of numbers maintained by previous highly restrictive policies on Asian immigration nor were the refugees destined for the same restricted social strata. Essentially, the admission of the refugees was the key factor in a process that finally blew the top off any possibility of identifying Australia as a transplanted piece of Europe.

As Viviani convincingly argues[21], this large-scale entry of refugees was not something that either Whitlam or Fraser wanted. Whitlam's policy on refugees was to be as restrictive of entry as possible. By

October 1975 only 1,034 had been admitted as permanent residents and although McKellar had ostensibly liberalized entry of refugees upon the conservatives' accession to power, in fact the insistence that potential entrants already have close family or other ties with Australia was an extremely restrictive one. By the end of 1977 only 4,909 had been admitted and McKellar firmly resisted increasing the Australian intake, at every step insisting on a 'possible backlash if large numbers of refugees were admitted'.[22]

In part the relatively small number of refugees admitted up to 1978 reflects a lull in refugee exodus from Indochina in the years 1976 and 1977. In 1978, however, the number of refugees increased dramatically and, as Viviani shows, the government was caught in a three-way pincer. First, public opinion on refugee entry was at best divided and in all probability for the most part hostile. Second, there was immense diplomatic pressure on the government to increase refugee intake from the USA and from the countries who became 'first arrival' destinations for refugees — Hong Kong, Malaysia, Thailand and the Phillipines. Third, the arrival in Darwin of a small number of boatloads of Vietnamese tapped into some very deep prejudices in the Australian population. In order to minimize the arrival of boat people in northern Australia, the co-operation of the South-East Asian countries was essential. The price for that was an accelerated programme of controlled refugee entry. Therefore McKellar and his department worked to establish a consensus of élite opinion favourable to refugee entry, one that would offset the political effects of a divided public opinion.[23]

By the early 1980s, then, the Fraser Government had changed the content of government ideology on race and ethnicity profoundly, and in ways which had enormous implications for Australian nationalism.

Multiculturalism and the ALP in the 1980s

We have pointed to the two very different sets of ideas and policies covered by the term 'multiculturalism': for the ALP in the Whitlam period, multiculturalism was a way of integrating migrants into general reformist welfare policies; for the Fraser Government, multiculturalism was an ideology to co-opt the leaders of ethnic organizations, while providing welfare on the cheap, through an ethnic group model. Both modes of multiculturalism were part of a process of construction of ethnic groups as a focal point of social cohesion and mobilization in Australia. The leaders of ethnic organizations were recognized by government as partners for consultation, and they were drawn into a wide range of advisory bodies. Funds for educational, welfare and cultural programmes were channelled through ethnic organizations, giving their functionaries the power that goes with patronage. The 'ethnic affairs units' or 'mul-

ticultural task forces' that were set up in a wide range of Commonwealth and State departments and agencies provided jobs for young
professionals, many of them first or second generation migrants.

Multiculturalism has thus moulded and consolidated its own constituency, which has in turn become a significant political lobby,
through its real or believed capacity to wield the 'ethnic vote'. This
factor explains the lack of clear direction in ALP policies since the
Hawke Government was elected in 1983. The natural inclination
would have been to return to generalist welfare policies of the type
developed under Whitlam — the slogan 'mainstreaming' (of which
more below) stands for this thrust. This has proved difficult for two
reasons: first, the economic crisis and the free-market solutions
adopted by the Hawke-Keating ministry have reduced the financial
leeway for improving, or even maintaining, welfare levels; second,
the ALP has fought shy of offending the multicultural lobby, and
has burnt its fingers when it has. The result has been a policy of
prevarication, which has done nothing to get to grips with the pressing problems of migrant workers in the economic crisis, nor to
combat New Right attacks on multiculturalism. Nor has the ALP
dealt effectively or creatively with the socio-cultural task of reducing
subtle racism and forging a wider sense of community in a multi-
ethnic context.

In its first two years, the Hawke Government essentially continued
the policies of the previous government, as laid down by the Galbally
Report. Stewart West (the only 'left' Cabinet Minister) was put at the
head of a very conservative department. There were some innova-
tions: a women's desk was established, grant-in-aid funding for community organizations was increased, and, for the first time, made
available to trade unions and workers' health centres. Measures to
improve equal opportunities and anti-discrimination legislation
benefited ethnic minorities, along with other groups. But there was
no basic change in policy.

The lack of direction became particularly evident with regard to
the issue of the future of the Australian Institute of Multicultural
Affairs (AIMA), which had been set up by the Fraser Government in
1980 to help implement the Galbally proposals. AIMA was widely
regarded as cut off from, and irrelevant to the needs of the ethnic
communities. Moreover, it was rapidly becoming a right-wing think
tank, with a leading role in the construction and diffusion of neo-
conservative ideologies.[24] For instance, AIMA had invited Michael
Nowak, Scholar in Residence of the American Enterprise Institute
and leading thinker of the 'new ethnicity' school, to Australia in
1982. Later, AIMA enlisted the Australian New Right figures Frank
Knopfelmacher and Robert Manne as commentators for its film
series 'The Migrant Experience'. West set up a Committee of Review
of AIMA. Its report, published late in 1983, was damning: the Insti-

tute was neither effective nor efficient, and had been a costly failure. Yet the federal Labor Government did not abolish AIMA, as was widely expected. On the contrary, it adopted a report containing a whole series of recommendations which had been submitted by AIMA to its Liberal predecessor. Apart from some cosmetic changes, such as new appointments to the Board, AIMA remained in business.

It became evident that no significant reform was planned in the ethnic affairs area — a fact which was underlined by the replacement of Stewart West by Chris Hurford as Minister. Hurford did not appear particularly interested in the portfolio, nor in developing close links with ethnic communities. His emphasis was on the administrative side of the department, and on linking immigration policies to the demands of employers for more migrant workers.

The development of a more specifically social-democratic form of multiculturalism came at this time not from the federal Government, but from the states. In 1977, the ALP Government of NSW had established the first Ethnic Affairs Commission (EAC). Although this had taken aboard some of the cultural baggage of the Zubrzycki-Galbally era, the EAC's founding document 'Participation' had laid the groundwork for a new approach. It asserted the duty of the government to provide equal access to its service for members of all ethnic groups, and to work for equal opportunities in society as a whole. The EAC was established as a government department, with the Premier, Neville Wran, taking on the portfolio of Ethnic Affairs. The thirteen Commissioners, appointed by the Premier, were to advise on the needs and problems of the ethnic communities, while the EAC was to have a general co-ordinating function, to ensure that all state government services and agencies were accessible to people of all ethnic groups. In addition to this monitoring role, the EAC took on research and policy tasks, and provided services such as interpreting and translating, aid in gaining recognition of overseas qualifications, and funding for ethnic organizations.

By the mid-1980s, the NSW EAC had over 80 employees and an annual budget of around $4m. Although tiny compared with the service delivery departments like health and education, it has had an impact on many areas of government. From 1984, all government departments and agencies were required to produce Ethnic Affairs Policy Statements (EAPS) to show what they were doing to make their services appropriate to the needs of various ethnic groups. Although implementation has proved slow, and many statements seem to be mere verbal declarations rather than indications of real change, the principle is important: multiculturalism has been officially designated as an element of all policies and services, rather than just a marginal extra to keep the 'ethnics' quiet. In NSW, the phrase 'mainstreaming' has been coined to refer to this: in the long run, all Galbally-type 'ethno-specific' services should be phased out, as 'mainstream' services are modified.

Further EACs have been established in the ALP-governed states South Australia (1980), Victoria (1983) and Western Australia (1984). Their structures and functions vary somewhat, but all are based on the idea of monitoring government services, and, where necessary, modifying them to be appropriate to a multicultural society. Yet at the same time, the EACs do deliver ethno-specific services, especially interpreting, translating and finance for ethnic groups. It is this last function which is often of most interest to community organizations, leading to conflicts when groups feel that they have received too little of the funding cake.

In 1985, policies on the Commonwealth level began to shift. In June of that year the government decided that all departments whose fields of work concerned migrants should provide an annual statement to the Minister for Immigration and Ethnic Affairs on measures taken to ensure 'access and equity'. These statements were clearly modelled on the NSW EAPS statements, though they appear to have had very little practical effect. At the end of 1985, the Minister for Immigration and Ethnic Affairs set up a 'Committee to Review Migrant and Multicultural Programmes and Services', chaired by James Jupp of the Australian National University. With very broad terms of reference, and a large research budget, this appeared — at last — to be an attempt to re-examine the whole area — in other words, to do a social democratic rewrite of Galbally.

But a mere return to the Whitlam social policy agenda was out of the question. As we argue elsewhere in this book, many of the conditions for such a policy had changed. To sum up the issues:

— A social democratic approach to multiculturalism meant moving away from ethno-specific services, but the financial constraints of the economic situation made any expansion of welfare or educational expenditure impossible. Cuts in ethno-specific services could thus not be fully compensated by general improvements.

— A growing body of research was providing ammunition for those in the bureaucracy who believed that 'ethnic disadvantage' was no longer an issue, and that inter-generational mobility was giving rise to a new middle class of second generation migrants who had no interest in ethnic issues.

— The new immigration policy advocated by Hurford, on the basis of demands by some employers and the Report of the Council for the Economic Development of Australia (CEDA), called for big increases in labour migration, as well as entry of entrepreneurs with capital. It was thought possible simultaneously to raise entries, and to cut post-arrival services and programmes, as market forces would take care of all problems in the long run.

— The Blainey Debate of 1984 had given rise to a widespread feeling that the multicultural lobby was losing ground, and that the 'ethnic vote' no longer counted. ALP strategists thought that multicultural sacred cows could be slaughtered without much protest. The slogan 'mainstreaming' thus took on a new meaning: ethno-specific services could be abolished and savings made by simply declaring that general services were now able to deal with the needs of the different ethnic groups. By the time the Jupp Committee submitted its weighty report in mid-1986[25], circumstances were changing rapidly in the run-up to the austerity budget of 1986-7. The first casualty was the AIMA. Having survived hostile reviews and the disenchantment of the ethnic communities, it had made efforts to become more relevant in 1985-6, carrying out two important research projects on the ethnic aged and ethnic youth, and organizing a national research conference. Now it was pre-emptively abolished. Severe cuts were made in funding for English as a Second Language (ESL) teaching, multicultural education in schools was slashed, and the National Professional Development programmes which played a crucial role in preparing teachers of migrant children was also abolished. The Government announced that the Special Broadcasting Service was to be merged with the ABC. Further cuts included the closure or scaling-down of regional offices of the Department of Immigration and Ethnic Affairs. The measures were generally received by the public as a retreat from multiculturalism, despite flustered denials from Hurford. Archbishop David Penman (Chairman of AIMA) summed up the feeling:

> The Government has dealt a dramatic and devastating blow to the future of Australia as a just and fair society. In a few key and highly selective measures the Government has abandoned multiculturalism completely — it has disappeared into our very own Bermuda Triangle.[26]

Had the Hawke Government decided to abandon multiculturalism in the belief that it was no longer necessary as an ideology to integrate the nation, and to co-opt ethnic leaderships? Some factors speak for this interpretation: the abandonment of pledges on Commonwealth Land Rights legislation, the dropping of the proposed Bill of Rights, the reorganization of the Human Rights Commission all indicate that such attempts at forging senses of community and ideological purpose were not only suspect but were seen as an expendable luxury in the economic crisis. Canberra insiders, on the other hand, argue that the draconian cuts in the multicultural area were the product of last-minute unco-ordinated bungling in the desperate attempt to find the required savings. Probably the truth lies in the middle.

Be that as it may, there is no doubt that the ALP strategists got it wrong. There was a speedy and emphatic reaction from the ethnic organizations, with public meetings, media statements and demonstrations held all over the country. The DIEA tried at first to belittle the reactions, then sent out observers to look for professional agitators. They found none — only migrant men and women concerned about their children's futures. Barry Unsworth, Premier of NSW, having narrowly won the election to the lower house seat of Rockdale, rushed to Canberra to tell Hawke that the ALP would lose both the federal and the NSW elections if damage-control measures were not instigated.

Unsworth was particularly influenced by reports that Muslim businessmen in certain Sydney electorates were able to influence strongly the voting behaviour of their co-religionists. However, there is no clear evidence to support this. No reliable surveys have demonstrated the existence of an 'ethnic vote'. Indeed, in view of the enormous political and social schisms within each ethnic group, not to speak of those between the various groups, it may be thought highly doubtful that there is any predictable controllable voting pattern of this kind. Nonetheless, measures which are widely seen as against the interests of ethnic communities, particularly in areas as close to people's concerns as education, might lead to spontaneous changes in voting behaviour. In addition, ethnic groups do have some influence on the parties through membership of local branches — in some industrial suburbs of the big cities, migrants may form the majority of ALP branches. So the point is not whether there is definitely an 'ethnic vote' or not, but that the risk of losing marginal seats through offending ethnic communities has become an important issue for the parties.

The result was another sudden about-turn in multicultural policies in late 1986 and early 1987. To start with, both Unsworth and Hawke henceforth lost no opportunity to press ethnic flesh, showing that they cared about the feelings of the leaderships constructed during the Galbally period. A new interpretation of history was launched, to convince people that the ALP had long been a conscious architect of multiculturalism. In the words of Bob Hawke:

> Some forty years ago, in the aftermath of war, the Labor Government led by Ben Chifley took a visionary, compassionate and historic decision. It opened the doors of Australia to a great wave of migration . . . It was a decision that allowed old cultures to flourish again in a new land, enriching and diversifying the Australian society. It was also a decision that provided a great new engine of manpower, a mass of workers whose energy, experience, and expertise helped build Australia's post-war prosperity to new levels.[27]

Some of the cuts in ESL funding were rescinded, albeit at the cost of other programmes for disadvantaged students. The SBS-ABC merger was withdrawn and a National Policy on Languages was adopted. The ethnic communities were explicitly spared any further cuts in the May 1987 Economic Statement. The key measure was the announcement by the Prime Minister of an Advisory Council on Multicultural Affairs (ACMA) and an Office of Multicultural Affairs (OMA). ACMA consists of prominent people, mainly of non-English speaking background. It is not a working body, but rather a sort of figurehead to mediate between government and the community. OMA, on the other hand is part of the Department of Prime Minister and Cabinet. In structure and tasks it is very like a state ethnic affairs commission. It will monitor Commonwealth Government policies and programmes (hopefully breathing life into the moribund 'access and equity statements'), advise on policy, carry out and commission research, and initiate programmes in community information and education. In other words, OMA will take up many of the functions of AIMA, but will be closer to real political power (and will probably cost more). ACMA and OMA together will work out a 'National Agenda for a Multicultural Australia', as announced by Bob Hawke in a speech to the ethnic communities in Melbourne on 26 April 1987.

A central aspect of this new policy is the emphasis on consultation. The principle of asking ethnic communities about their needs and wishes was introduced under Whitlam, developed by Galbally, and institutionalized in the ethnic affairs commissions. OMA now actually has a 'division of consultation'. This sounds very democratic, but has its problems: in a representative parliamentary system, the people are supposed to be the fount of all power, which is delegated to parliament and the government through the electoral process. Consultation short circuits this: the government asks people directly, but it decides who it is going to ask, and whether it is going to take any notice of what they say. Clearly, government has the opportunity of consulting only those who say what it wants to hear. Consultation becomes a new form of patronage, bolstering the power of ethnic leaders and functionaries of recognized organizations. Groups or organizations not officially regarded as worthy of being consulted are pushed out of the political process. Currently, consultation looks set to become a new fetish to legitimate government policies, as well as an instrument for postponing action.

So the wheel seems to have turned full circle in just one year. Evidently the ALP has discovered that it cannot cope without the rhetoric of multiculturalism, and that the rhetoric does not come free of charge: it must be accompanied by measures to meet the expectations of ethnic leaderships. But the ethnic communities have been alerted to the superficial character of multicultural ideology. It was not an issue of principle for the ALP: when it was regarded as expendable, multiculturalism was thrown overboard, and it was restored only because of the feared electoral consequences. There is much mistrust of ACMA and OMA in ethnic organizations, particularly those concerned with the employment situation, health, education and the welfare of migrant workers. In particular, there is a strong feeling that the 'National Agenda' is a simple way of postponing decisions, for it is expected to take over two years to work out. It will be ready just before the next federal election.

Multiculturalism remains an ambiguous and ephemeral phenomenon in Australian politics. It has become a necessary ideology, and has created its own constituency and institutional basis. Yet neither of the major parties has a clear idea of the way ahead in this area. The ALP would like to merge multicultural programmes and services into a general (and reduced) welfare system, but finds it cannot do so without the rhetoric and the institutions necessary to maintain it. The Liberals have moved away from many of the principles which made their adoption of multiculturalism possible in the late 1970s. Their current concepts of policies in this area seem to relate to the celebration of cultural diversity and the encouragement of ethnic small business, but it is quite unclear what this would mean in practice.

How have mass immigration and Aboriginal claims changed Australian society by the late 1980s? In structural terms, there has been a considerable degree of incorporation of immigrants, not just into a stratum of poorly paid and unpleasant employment, but a degree of upward socio-economic mobility, too. Despite the rhetoric of multiculturalism, the fundamental and sociological reality is incorporation into the institutional structures of an advanced industrial society and many of its intrinsic cultural values, too: consumerism, competition, trade union values, etc. Apart from a growing number of government-sponsored welfare workers, the Aboriginal socioeconomic presence, on the other hand, is mostly to be characterized as one of exclusion, of marginalization from the most basic economic and political structures of contemporary Australian society.

Australian governments, in response to the effects of mass immigration and Aboriginal claims, have moved towards a policy of cultural pluralism. Despite fundamental sociological realities of structural incorporation/exclusion, they have aimed to reconstruct the issue simply as one of maintaining, supporting and celebrating cultural difference. Respect, tolerate, even support the differences, and cultural autonomy and equality of opportunity will supposedly be ensured. This move occurred through a developing, mutually supporting relationship between leaderships ostensibly representing their specific constituency, and the government, constructing particular leaderships as specifically 'ethnic', funding semi-volunteer education and welfare servicing, and redefining Australia as a site of cultural diversity rather than as an economic and cultural monolith. The visible manifestation of this socio-cultural move is a political and national imagery of multiculturalism, which is founded upon the grassroots of immigrant or Aboriginal political demands and which at the same time reconstructs these demands into a 'cultural' constituency by patterns of state funding and ideological direction. In the process there emerged a powerful 'ethnic' lobby, and a less powerful Aboriginal lobby, demanding both specialist servicing in the interests of social participation and equity, and rights of cultural maintenance and autonomy. The national imagery of multiculturalism is manifest in officially supported cultural activities and events: carnival, 'ethnic' or Aboriginal heritage through song, dance and food displays, and so on.

Having analysed the sociological and historical bases for the rise of multiculturalism, we will return in Chapters Six and Seven to examine these fundamental questions of culture, identity and politics. But first, in the following chapter, we set Australia in an international-comparative context.

Notes

1. A.C. Palfreeman, 'The White Australia policy' in: F. Stevens (ed.), *Racism, the Australian Experience*, Brookvale: ANZ Book Company 1971, p.169.
2. *Hansard* 20 March 1974, p.649.
3. C. Cameron, *Hansard* 14 November 1974, p.3524.
4. J. Martin, *The Migrant Presence*, Sydney: George Allen & Unwin 1978, p.55.
5. A. J. Grassby, *A Multi-Cultural Society for the Future*, Immigration Reference Paper, Australia, Department of Immigration, Canberra: AGPS 1973.
6. G. Whitlam quoted in Jakubowicz, Morrissey and Palser, 1970, p.45.
7. Jean Martin, p.50.
8. *Ibid*
9. Lippman 1979 quoted in Jakubowicz, Morrissey and Palser, p.45.
10. Martin, p.57.
11. Australian Ethnic Affairs Council (Chairman: J. Zubrzycki), *Australia as a Multicultural Society*, Canberra: 1977, p.17-18. Our emphasis.
12. A. Faulkner and D.Storer, 'The Georgiou Report', *Migration Action* Vol:1, 1982.
13. Jakubowicz, Morrissey and Palser, *passim*.
14. Galbally, *Review of Port-Arrival Programmes and Services to Migrants*, Canberra: AGPS 1978.
15. *Ibid*.
16. *Ibid*, p.110.
17. *Ibid*.
18. *Ibid*.
19. For detailed treatment of this topic, see Jakubowicz, Morrissey and Palser, pp.81ff.
20. N. Viviani, *The Long Journey: Vietnamese Migration and Settlement in Australia*, Melbourne University Press 1984, p.85.

21.   *Ibid*, pp.82-127.
22.   *Ibid*, p.87.
23.   *Ibid*, p.114.
24.   See, Jakubowicz, Morrissey and Palser, pp.89ff; and A. Jakubowicz, 'Ethnicity, multiculturalism and neo-conservatism' in: G. Bottomley and M. de Lepervanche (eds), *Ethnicity, Class and Gender in Australia*, Sydney: George Allen & Unwin 1984, passim.
25.   *Don't Settle for Less — Report of the Committee for Stage 1 of the Review of Migrant and Multicultural Programs and Services*, Canberra: AGPS 1986.
26.   AIMA *Press Release*, 20 August 1986.
27.   Speech to ethnic communities Melbourne, 26 April 1987.

5.
Labour Migration, Racism and the Nation — International Perspectives

Migrant labour and economic development

This chapter aims to provide an international context for understanding the Australian situation. We will look at general aspects of the use of migrant labour, and of the role of racial/ethnic boundaries in constructing nationalism; we will also examine the specific features of Western European and North American countries, in comparison with Australia. We start with an analysis of the function of migrant labour for advanced western economies in the post-war growth period. We then look at the changing situation of the new ethnic minorities in the period of recession and restructuring. There follows a description of the changing character of racism, and its role in the construction of national senses of solidarity.

Large-scale use of migrant labour has been a feature of most advanced economies since 1945.[1] There is nothing new about this: industrialization involves the concentration of materials, machinery and workers at new sites of production, and hence has always involved labour migration. Initially this generally takes the form of internal rural-urban movements, but throughout the history of industrial development employers have found it necessary to overcome the limitations of national labour resources by organizing or encouraging the entry of workers from abroad. The key role of Irish 'navvies'[2] in the British industrial revolution is a well-known early example.

The use of migrant labour is not simply a question of providing *additional* workers to fuel production, consumption and capital formation, it is also connected with the *specific characteristics* of migrants: lack of education, skills and language proficiency may force migrants to take low-status jobs that locals reject. This may be reinforced by racial and ethnic divisions which keep migrants out of certain sectors; or by the desperation of entrants from impoverished or war-torn areas, who will take any employment they can get. So migrant workers may be used for dirty and dangerous jobs, or to work in remote areas, or to do shift and night work. Migrant labour has thus often played a role in employers' strategies for structural change, involving greater control of the labour force and de-skilling. Migration is frequently used to regulate the labour market by influencing levels of wages and profits. Full employment allows workers and unions to obtain better wages and conditions. In response, employers seek measures to restore the 'flexibility' of the labour market, by which they mean creating a pool of unemployed persons. In this sense, potential migrants in peripheral low-wage areas of the world may serve as an 'industrial reserve army', helping to maintain profitability in the more advanced sectors.[3] Since industrialization, the regulation of labour migration has been a crucial role of the nation-state.

The use of migrant labour often involves a contradiction within the ideology of the free market economy in which the potential worker is supposed to be a free individual. Migrant workers frequently lack the freedom to make a contract with employers on an equal legal footing. Typically they are admitted to the country only on certain conditions, concerning type and duration of work, restrictions on residence, civil and political rights, and so on. Migrant workers are, to an extent, 'unfree' workers. They suffer legal disabilities which exclude them from certain jobs, or bind them to others. In other words, they do not have the freedom to compete equally on the labour market. The legal disabilities of migrant workers are generally laid down on the basis of exclusionary criteria, linked to nationality, race or citizenship. These may be seen as particular forms of structural racism.

In fact, the use of 'unfree' labour is to be found in various forms, of which migrant labour is just one, throughout the history of world capitalist development. Slavery in the plantations of America and the Carribean provided substantial capital for the industrial revolutions in Britain, France and other European countries. 'Parish apprentices' (like Oliver Twist) were forced to work in Britain's early mines and factories. The 'industrial schools' and 'workhouses' of France and Germany were used to exploit the labour of destitute children and adults. Convict labour was crucial to the early development of Australia. The Nazis used up to seven million forced labourers, including slave-workers in the concentration camps, in their war economy. The modern South African economy is based on a rigid system of worker exploitation and racial exclusion.

The use of 'unfree' labour is advantageous to employers in two ways: first, it allows the payment of low wages to the workers concerned, and makes it hard for them to demand better conditions; second, it causes splits within the workforce, and weakens the unity of trade unions. For instance, the use of Polish workers as strike breakers and cheap labour was an overt policy of the German employers and Imperial State before the First World War.[4] The reaction of local workers to such policies has often been to oppose labour migration and to demand state action to safeguard the rights and conditions of the existing labour force.

This 'rational' defensive posture has often taken on the character of racism towards the migrant workers themselves, for example, towards the Irish in nineteenth-century Britain, towards the Poles in Germany before the First World War, towards non-white workers in Australia during and after the Gold Rush, towards post-Second World War black immigrants in France and Britain. When we look at such historical examples it is difficult to distinguish clearly between the attempt to safeguard working-class conditions by preventing dilution of labour, and racial discrimination against non-whites and foreigners. The contradiction arises because the white working classes of the advanced industrial countries have for centuries been imbued with the racist stereotypes of colonialism and imperialism. Racism has roots deep within popular culture and traditions. As an ideology, its core of 'rationality' lies in the fact that colonial exploitation did at times benefit the working classes of imperialist countries, giving them, in Engels' words, the position of a labour aristocracy.[5]

In the New World context, the history of ideologies and practices of racism towards potentially threatening immigrant 'others' is compounded by the direct experience of expropriating the land of indigenous peoples. In the Australian case Aborigines were the victims of ruthless and violent forms of racism. These were linked both to the thoroughness of their exclusion by the Europeans, and their own cultural disdain and distance from the frontier European society they saw at first hand. But the basis of this racism was fundamentally different from that practised against culturally different immigrants. The Aborigines simply did not constitute the same sort of threat. Despite this difference in context and intent, a racist narrative developed in order to rationalize one event is eminently transferrable to another, albeit very different event. In other words, New World racism took particular and virulent forms as a result of the immediacy of its experience of decimating indigenous people. Racist propaganda depicting Aboriginal-European difference was in a large part transferrable to the 'difference' of Chinese immigrants during the Gold Rush period in nineteenth-century Australia.

Migration and the post-1945 boom

All the major industrial countries of Western Europe, as well as the USA, Canada and Australia, experienced mass immigration in the post-1945 period. (Japanese expansion has also been based to some extent on the use of Korean minority workers, although the scale seems to have been smaller than in other countries.) The forms, volume and timing of the migrations have varied.

The main forms are the following:

1. Colonial administrators and settlers returning to former colonial powers (Britain, France, Belgium, the Netherlands). This does not lead to formation of ethnic minorities, but may well affect attitudes towards them (e.g. the *pieds noirs* — the returnees from Algeria — play a big part in racist movements in France).

2. Refugees. There was a major problem of resettlement of displaced persons after the Second World War. A reduction in refugee intakes in the 1950s and 1960s was followed by an increase affecting all developed countries in the aftermath of upheavals in the 1970s and 1980s. Unlike labour migrants, refugees are for the most part not selected to meet the economic interests of the receiving country, and are, therefore, often particularly vulnerable to unemployment and exploitation. Entries of refugees may have a substantial effect on public attitudes, affecting non-refugee migrants too (e.g. the East African Asians in Britain in the mid-1970s, the Vietnamese in Australia, African and Asian refugees in West Germany at present.)

3. Colonial workers — labour migrants from colonies or former colonies entering the 'mother country'. This applies mainly to Britain, France and the Netherlands (although Puerto Ricans moving to the USA might also be included). Such migrants generally have had the citizenship of the country of immigration, but have, on the other hand been visibly distinguishable, generally by skin colour.

4. Migrant workers from areas on the periphery of industrial development, such as Southern Europeans, Turks and North Africans moving to Western Europe, Mexicans moving to the USA, and New Zealanders entering Australia. This is by far the biggest single category of migrants, and has several sub-divisions:

— Workers migrating within free movement systems, such as the European Common Market or the Nordic Labour Market, which guarantee labour market rights and social benefits. Movement between New Zealand and Australia is similar.

— Migrants recruited as temporary contract labour within 'guest-worker' systems. These have been used by virtually all Western European countries. Typically, the rights of such workers to long-term residence, social benefits, family reunification and political participation have been severely restricted by special

legislation. Nevertheless, many of these temporary workers have become settlers.[6]
— Illegal immigrants, who have come in search of work, without documentation. This applies to virtually all countries, most particularly to France and the USA. For many employers, the 'illegal' is the dream worker, for lack of legal status makes him/her extremely vulnerable to exploitation. Often legal migrants get pushed into illegality, when their status is eroded by unemployment.
— Seasonal workers, used extensively in agriculture in the USA and France, and in a wide range of occupations in Switzerland. Often seasonal status is merely a device to deny migrants rights.
— Frontier workers, used extensively in Switzerland. Such workers, who cross national frontiers on their daily journey to work, are another category with very restricted rights.
5. Permanent settlers, whose immigration is encouraged for demographic or population-building reasons, e.g. in the case of Australia, Canada and the USA. However, such migrants do not always stay permanently, whatever the original intention. Often the distinction between this category and the previous one is not a rigid one: the policy of 'populate or perish' does not preclude the use of migrants as 'factory fodder'.

The volume of the post-war migrations has been very large: about 30 million workers and their dependants entered Western Europe in the post-war period; about five and a half million migrants entered Australia from 1945 to 1982.[7] Of course not all of them stayed: altogether about 16 million people in Western Europe today are migrants or children of migrants (and this is a minimum estimate, excluding those who have become naturalized).[8] Migrants make up 5 to 10 per cent of the populations of most countries (14 per cent in the case of Switzerland). In Australia, the 1981 Census showed that three million people were overseas born (21 per cent of the total population). Just under three million (20 per cent) had at least one overseas-born parent — i.e. they were second-generation migrants. Foreign-born people make up about 15 per cent of the population of Canada, and about 5 per cent of the population of the USA. Nett migration to Canada has been between 80,000 and 120,000 annually in recent years. Entries to the USA have fluctuated between 350,000 and 600,000 per year.[9] The post-Second World War migrations have been among the greatest in human history; their impact on society is unsurprising.

The timing of the migrations is perhaps the clearest indicator of their link to the extraordinary post-war economic boom. Labour migration was concentrated overwhelmingly in the period 1945 to 1973, in the expansive long wave of the world economy. Migration has declined considerably in volume since the mid-1970s and in the rest of the world as in Australia, its character has shifted away from labour migration to family reunion and refugee movement. In the subsequent stagnation and restructuring, labour migration to advanced countries has for the most part stopped (the USA is an exception), and there have even been trends towards repatriation in some cases. This general picture needs to be filled in briefly for various areas.

Western Europe

Most industrial countries recruited labour from 1945 onwards, at first for post-war reconstruction, later to sustain the emerging boom. Only West Germany started significantly later (about 1956), because there were large internal reserves, as well as German refugees from the East. In most countries labour migration continued into the early 1970s, actually reaching its highest levels towards the end of the period. (Here the exception is Britain, where most labour migration was stopped by the 1962 Commonwealth Immigrants Act. The causes were both economic — the early beginning of stagnation — and political — the emergence of racial conflict in the 1950s).

In all the countries concerned, the state played a significant role either in the recruitment of migrant labour, or in the regulation of its labour market, social and political status or in both. State policies were nowhere based on long-term planning, but rather on short-term responses to employers' labour requirements, and (later) on attempts to cope with emerging social, political and public order problems. It is important to examine the difference between situations where a large proportion of migrants have been of the 'guestworker' type, and those where many migrants have come from colonies. In the former case, there is a system of institutionalized discrimination, regarded as legitimate by most social groups; in the latter, migrants have citizenship, and discrimination is less formalized. However, it should be noted that there has been a clear trend towards convergence in the legal frameworks relating to these two types of migrants over the last 20 years.

In the 1950s and 1960s, most labour migrants came to Western Europe from neighbouring areas: Southern Europeans to France, Belgium, Switzerland, Germany; Irish to Britain; Finns to Sweden. Migration of non-Europeans from the colonies and former colonies also got under way, but was smaller in volume. In the 1970s and 1980s, many Southern European 'guestworkers' have returned home, while new entries have been from more distant, Third World areas: Turks, North Africans and Latin American, African and Asian refugees. A trend towards family reunion has turned the 'guestworkers', and particularly those from the Third World, into new and permanent ethnic minorities. In the three biggest countries of immigration,

France, West Germany and Britain, about 40 per cent of the ethnic minority population (around two million people in each case) are non-European. This growth of Third World immigration applies to North America and Australia as well, as will be shown below.

The USA

The situation with regard to migration and racial/ethnic divisions is particularly complex here. The USA is a society very consciously built upon immigration. After the violent conquest of the indigenous peoples, the main division was to be that between black and white, originating in the forced recruitment of slave labour for the plantations in the seventeenth, eighteenth and nineteenth centuries. Lincoln's Emancipation Proclamation of 1863 improved only temporarily the lot of the black population: soon slavery was replaced by the 'Jim Crow System' of rigid segregation, enforced by lynchings. After 1900 the mass migrations from the rural Deep South to the industrial cities of the North, the Middle West and California turned many blacks from peasants to industrial workers. But it took the Freedom Rides and the ghetto risings of the 1960s to make racism and exclusion of blacks a major political issue. Even today, despite the growth of a visible black middle class, the majority of Afro-Americans are still highly disadvantaged in economic and social terms.[10]

Between 1820 and 1920, about 33 million immigrants, mostly from Europe, entered the USA.[11] The streams of newcomers, who were welcomed by the Statue of Liberty in New York Harbour, provided the labour force for the USA's industrial take-off, as well as forming the raw material for the pluralist ideology of the 'melting pot'. Mass immigration from overseas was stopped in the 1920s. It was the blacks from the South who provided the factory fodder after that, until the Great Depression killed labour demand for a while.

After the Second World War, immigration resumed. Legal entries averaged 251,000 per year in the period 1951-60, 332,000 per year from 1961-70, 449,000 per year from 1971-80 and 573,000 per year from 1981-5. Though large in absolute numbers, this immigration has added less than one-quarter of a per cent to US population in any one year. In the 1950s about 60 per cent of immigrants came from Europe. By the 1980s, the European share had fallen to 10 per cent. From 1981-5, 12 per cent of legal migrants came from Mexico, 22 per cent from other Latin American countries and 40 per cent from Asia.[12]

The USA has not followed policies of state labour recruitment and legal migrants have been regarded as potential permanent citizens. The state has done little to ease settlement, nor to regulate the conditions of immigrants — factors that have all been left to market forces. Yet certain groups have had a role similar to that of the 'guest-

workers' or colonial migrants in Europe. Immigrants from less developed areas, particularly those of different skin colour or appearance, have tended to get the least desirable jobs in manufacturing
and the services. This applies to Carribean and Latin American immigrants and to some Asian groups. Unlike Western Europe, where
the states stopped labour migration and attempted to export unemployment when the recession started, the US Government has not
stopped immigration at times of high unemployment. Indeed, we
may witness the paradox of extremely high rates of black unemployment, while new Latin American and Asian migrants come in large
numbers, and get the new jobs being created in the process of industrial restructuring. This is because the new migrants go where there is
work, and, lacking welfare rights, have no choice but to take jobs,
however exploitative the conditions.

The great difference in wage levels between the USA and Mexico
has given rise to large-scale illegal migration across the 3,000 km
long border. US agri-business employers systematically exploit the
labour of the 'wetbacks' who cross the Rio Grande, and the border
patrols only go through the motions of trying to stop this movement.
Most illegal migrants lack skills and education, and are extremely
vulnerable because of their lack of legal protection. The number of
illegals is estimated to be between three and six million. After years
of debate, the Immigration Reform and Control Act of 1986 granted
an amnesty to illegal aliens who had lived continuously in the USA
since 1 January 1982, or who had worked in seasonal agriculture for
at least 90 days in the year ending 1 May 1986. It is expected that
three to four million illegals will qualify for legal status. Once they
gain 'permanent resident' status, or citizenship, they will be able to
sponsor relatives for entry. This is expected to lead to an increase in
low-skilled immigrants in coming years, providing a labour reserve
for low-paid jobs. At the same time, some groups of Asian migrants
provide more highly-skilled labour, or entrepreneurial experience for
the small business sector.

Canada

Like the USA and Australia, Canada is a traditional country of immigration, where policies have aimed at population-building, and
not just labour recruitment. Historically, Canada has had a complex
ethnic situation. The dispossessed original inhabitants have led a
marginalized and discriminated life. Colonization by both Britain
and France has led to a division among the white population, with
marked linguistic and cultural conflicts. Immigration was at high
levels in the immediate post-war period, reaching nearly 200,000 in
1951. The overwhelming majority came from Europe. Immigration
declined in the 1950s, bottoming out at 72,000 in 1961. Immigration
increased again in the 1960s, with most migrants coming from the

USA (many were Vietnam draft resisters), the West Indies and Asia. By 1981 only 15 per cent of the 129,000 new entrants were from the UK, 7 per cent from the USA and 20 per cent from other European countries. Forty per cent were from Asia and 13 per cent from other American countries, mainly the West Indies.[13]

Australia

Post-war migration policy was based on both population and labour market needs, with the state playing a substantial role in the recruitment and selection of migrants. The original intention to recruit predominantly from the British Isles had to be abandoned, as there were not enough applicants. Migrants came from areas of increasing cultural distance: first Eastern Europe, then Southern Europe, the Middle East and Asia. Migrants from the UK and Eire have remained the largest single group, but their share has dropped from 43 per cent in the 1959-70 period to 29 per cent in the 1970-81 period. Migrant intakes were reduced substantially as the boom ended in the early 1970s: there was a nett settler gain of 1.3 million between 1959 and 1970, but of only 545,000 from 1970 to 1981. At the same time the emphasis shifted from 'general eligibility' (mainly economically active migrants) to family reunion and refugees. In 1984-5, the total migrant intake was 69,486, of whom 39,485 (57 per cent) came under the category family migration and 14,207 (20 per cent were refugees).[14] However, the most recent trend has been to increase migrant intakes to about 120,000 per year and to emphasize the economic benefits of bringing in both immigrant workers and business people, who are required to bring with them a minimum of $150,000 for local investment.

Economic structure and migration

We argued above that migrant workers were recruited not only because additional labour was needed in the boom period, but also because migrants provided a specific type of labour, and because systems of informal and institutional discrimination turned migrants into semi-unfree labour. This general hypothesis needs linking to structural development during the long boom. To put it briefly; the conditions for growth of the old industrial countries were extremely good after the Second World War. The dominance of the US economy allowed a restructuring of world financial and commodity markets. US capital reorganized large sections of production in Western Europe. Decolonization and the increasing economic dependence of emerging Third World countries secured cheap raw materials. There were abundant labour supplies. The weakening of traditional trade union concerns and claims through fascism and war (especially in the later 'economic miracle' countries of West

Germany, Italy and Japan) helped to keep wages low relative to productivity growth. Profits were therefore high, and investment paid off. Demand for goods of all kinds was also high, due to wartime reconstruction needs, then later due to rearmament in the Cold War, and to the beginnings of the mass consumption boom.

The import of migrant labour started at first to meet specific bottlenecks (for example, in the mines in Belgium, in agriculture in France), but rapidly spread across all sectors, in response to full employment. As a section of the indigenous labour force was able to take advantage of opportunities for upward mobility provided by economic growth, migrants were brought in to fill the poorly-paid, heavy, unhealthy low-skill jobs. They were forced into these jobs both by their lack of marketable capabilities (education, vocational training or language proficiency), and by labour market discrimination. The latter had two principal forms: informal racism, particularly against non-Europeans (such as colonial migrants), and structural racism (which applied particularly to the 'guestworkers').

By the 1960s, the conditions for economic expansion were no longer as positive. Full employment allowed wage growth, which reduced profitability of investments; that is, wages grew and profits declined as a percentage of Gross National Product. International competition in industrial production increased, and demand for some commodities became more sluggish. The US and British economies moved into stop-go cycles of 'stagflation' (simultaneous high rates of unemployment and inflation) and even West Germany experienced its first significant recession in 1966-8.

New strategies were then sought to restore growth, principally by increasing the productivity of labour. These were based partly on technological change, but even more on reorganization of the labour process: that is, on the introduction of conveyor-line production, large-series manufacture, continuous-process production, shift-work, piece-work and premium payment systems. This involved not only getting more production per worker, but also de-skilling the work-force by breaking up jobs into small, repetitive tasks. There was a trend towards polarization of the workforce, with a small group of very-highly trained technicians and tradespeople on the one hand, and an increasing army of semi-skilled process workers on the other. The latter were replaceable and therefore easily controllable. This is the explanation for the great upsurge in the recruitment of migrant labour from the mid-1960s to the early 1970s. The use of migrants in a situation of expansion matches the need for de-skilling and controlling the workforce. In West Germany, for instance, the migrant labour force increased from 900,000 at the end of the recession in 1968, to 2.6 million by 1973 — over 300,000 additional migrant workers per year. Developments in France were similar. In Australia, too, migrant workers played a significant part in the attempt to shift the emphasis of the economy from primary products to manufacturing in this period.

Migrant labour in the economic recession

In 1973-4, intakes of migrant workers were drastically cut everywhere (except for North America). In Western Europe, states expected and encouraged return migration, but, as already mentioned, most migrant workers stayed, brought in their families and became permanent settlers. In the boom period, migrants' role was primarily economic, and the state was concerned with satisfying short-term labour requirements. In the subsequent recession years, migrants still have an important economic role (which we shall examine in this section), but this has been joined by an ideological role, linked with attempts to maintain the legitimacy of the nation-state, through the reassertion of nationalism. It is in the drawing of the exclusionary boundaries of the nation that racism takes on key significance. That will be the theme of the next section.

The starting point for understanding the current economic role of migrants and ethnic minorities is to look at the structural changes which have led to the termination of migrant labour recruitment for the old industrial centres. The 'oil crisis' of 1973 triggered the measures to stop migration, and appeared as the harbinger of the period of stagnation. The subsequent period has shown, however, that much deeper factors were at work. Industrial production was becoming less and less profitable in the old industrial areas. To put it simply: the concentration of industry in very small areas (particularly the triangle with its corners at Birmingham, Hamburg and Turin) led to an upsurge in the costs of the production factors: labour was scarce and expensive; the cost of labour-saving investments was soaring; land costs were becoming astronomical. The concentration of so much industry in such a small area destroyed the natural environment, making pollution controls inevitable, further raising production costs. The strategy of mass production and increased productivity brought only a temporary respite.

From the early 1970s new approaches were needed, and these appeared as a reversal of the previous trends: the Western European countries which had hitherto imported capital and labour now started exporting capital, and shifting labour-intensive work processes to low-wage Third World countries. US, West European and Japanese capital became increasingly trans-national, producing in the Carribean, Latin America, Asia, North Africa and even Eastern Europe.[15] The de-skilling of certain labour processes was a pre-condition for this trend, which in turn made labour migration to the advanced countries superfluous.

The 'new international division of labour' is just one aspect of the current world economy. Within the old industrial centres the remaining production processes are being transformed by the use of electronic methods of control and organization. These are changing the job content and working conditions of large sections of the workforce, and often reducing the numbers of jobs available. Changes in the products and the ways they are made alters demand for specific types of skills, as well as for various types of raw materials (a particularly important factor for primary producer countries, and for traditional heavy industries). Rapid improvements in communications and data processing increase the integration of the world economy and the dominance of huge trans-national corporations. The control of world production and exchange is becoming increasingly concentrated in a few world financial centres: 'global cities' like London, Frankfurt, New York, Los Angeles, Tokyo, Singapore and Sydney.

The concentration of 'global control capability'[16] gives a new dimension to the polarization of the labour force: such cities require a large number of highly-educated specialists for financial control, management, planning, design and research, but these highly-paid corporate and state employees in turn generate a large demand for consumer goods and services. So there is also a demand for low-skilled decentralized labour in such centres. Manufacturing industry can be resited in low-wage areas, but buildings and services have to be produced where they are to be used.

Three situations appear typical of the role of migrant or minority labour in this new social and economic context. First, the majority of migrant workers remain employed in manufacturing, construction and certain service areas. Although employment in these areas has declined, the high concentration of migrants in certain occupations — generally those with poor working conditions, a dangerous working environment and low pay and status — means they cannot easily be replaced by unemployed indigenous workers. Certain mass production sectors, such as car assembly (mainly male workers), or electrical goods assembly (mainly female workers), are still generally staffed by migrants. In theory, it would be possible to force unemployed indigenous workers to take such jobs, but in practice the political and social costs of such measures have kept them at a minimum.

Second, a large proportion of those migrant workers who have been displaced from formal employment remain in the country of immigration as a floating and marginalized potential labour force. They live on the dole, or on the resources of the family. The burden of supporting unemployment is often transferred from the state to the migrant family. This applies particularly in countries like West Germany where unemployed migrants may lose their right to residence and become illegal under certain circumstances. Even going on the official statistics, which under-numerate unemployed migrants, their rate of unemployment is everywhere higher than that of nationals.[17] As young migrants (the 'second generation') try to enter the labour market, they are particularly vulnerable to unemployment. In many cases the education system has failed to provide them with the knowledge, capabilities and certificates needed to have a chance under current conditions, so they have particularly high unemployment rates.[18]

Third, migrants play a significant part in the trend towards decentralization of production and service provision mentioned above. Small businesses and home-working involve migrants both as workers and as entrepreneurs. Such enterprises appear marginal, but actually are often linked to large-scale capital in complex chains of sub-contracting. Luxury services, such as restaurants, are disproportionately provided by migrants, with a high degree of utilization of women's and family labour power. The informal sector, based on special exploitation of migrants', women's and young people's labour is the flip-side of the concentration of the great transnational corporations (and of state employment) in the global cities.[19]

Clearly, these three aspects are closely related: the migrant expelled from formal employment due to manufacturing restructuring may oscillate between unemployment and irregular work in the informal sector. Where global control capability becomes concentrated, and there is a high demand for goods and services, new migrants may be drawn in. This would appear to be the explanation for the continued large-scale migration from overseas to the cities of the USA, despite high levels of unemployment.

Racism and recession

During the period of mass labour recruitment from 1945 to the mid-1970s, popular attitudes towards migrants varied. Colonial migrants were for the most part treated according to stereotypes of racial inferiority, and discriminated against on the basis of colour. Southern Europeans recruited as 'guestworkers' in Western Europe were treated as culturally inferior, but accepted in a patronizing way as being economically necessary.[20] The institutional racism of 'guestworker' systems reflected a widespread readiness to accept discrimination against migrants as normal: employers, unions, the media and welfare organizations did little or nothing to question the principle of denying rights to non-citizen workers. The policy of assimilation in Australia, designed to turn labour migrants into permanent settlers, appears at first sight to be the very opposite of such 'guestworker' policies. But it was also based on the labelling of non-Anglo cultures as inferior and even harmful, on the expectation that these would disappear. Racism against blacks and other non-Europeans in the USA has been a pervading and continuous social phenomenon.

There is ample evidence that racism has continued and, in some cases, grown in intensity, since the mid-1970s. At the same time, we would argue, the character of racism has changed.

In Western Europe, racist stereotypes play an increasing part in popular attitudes, taking the form of jokes, remarks and everyday behaviour, and motivating discrimination. Opinion polls in Britain, France, West Germany and other countries show a steady increase in anti-immigrant attitudes. Many people appear to blame foreign workers or black people for economic and social problems, and to support policies of immigration control, restriction of rights and even repatriation. The extreme right has been quick to take advantage of this mood. Declining real wages, growing unemployment, decline of traditional industries and the decay of working-class housing areas have led to an atmosphere of discontent and hopelessness, particularly among working-class youth. Neo-fascist groups like the National Front and the British Movement have mobilized white youth with slogans which play on working-class fears of competition for jobs, housing and social amenities. The result has been an escalation of racially-motivated violence in cities throughout Western Europe, with assault, vandalism, arson and even murder becoming frequent.[21]

The extreme right has had a two-pronged strategy: systematic racist terrorism has been linked with propaganda campaigns designed to gain entry into parliament and local government. There are close links between the neo-fascist terrorist fringe, and the legal, parliamentary extreme right. In France this strategy has paid off: the *Front National* got around 10 per cent of the vote in the parliamentary elections of 1986, and now constitutes a powerful political force. In West Germany and Britain extreme right groups have had little enduring electoral success, in part because of the way the electoral systems of these countries are structured. Here the emphasis of extreme-right activities has remained on street violence.

Perhaps the most threatening aspect of such developments has been their impact on mainstream politics. Politicians of major parties of the centre-right have gradually shifted their ground to take up racist themes. Even the traditionally more progressive parties have not been immune to this. In France, communist mayors have led anti-North African demonstrations. In West Germany, leading social democrats have been reluctant to adopt policies to improve the situation of foreign workers for fear of an electoral backlash in working-class areas.[22] In most West European countries, politicians and the media have defined migrants as 'the foreigner problem' which poses a threat to economic well-being and social peace.[23] This applies particularly to second generation immigrant youth, who are frequently referred to as a 'social time-bomb'. A similar discourse in British politics goes back to Enoch Powell's inflammatory speeches (evoking 'rivers of blood') in the 1960s. Racist categories remain firmly entrenched in Tory thinking.[24]

In the USA, the ghetto riots and the civil rights movement initiated an era of legislation and action to combat racism. Between 1954 and 1968 there were six major legislative and judicial acts designed to elevate the citizenship status of Afro-Americans.[25] But in the 1970s and 1980s there has been a reaction against such trends, and overt racism has reasserted itself. Surveying a wide range of research findings, Pinkney found that white attitudes towards blacks in the USA did change for the better in recent decades, but that in some areas, whites still maintained strongly negative attitudes towards blacks.[26] He also found a high degree of discrimination and institutional racism in the economy, in education, in the administration of justice and in health care. The 1980 US Census showed that the median family income of blacks is only 58 per cent of that of whites. Blacks are still under-represented in high-status occupations, and their unemployment rates have been consistently twice as high as those of whites.[27]

The situation of the many other minority groups in US society is too complex to deal with adequately here. The indigenous peoples, as in Australia, have achieved neither cultural autonomy nor equity within the structures of industrial society established in the centuries since their conquest. Some of the earliest white immigrant groups, such as the Irish and the Jews, experienced both racial stereotyping and widespread discrimination. Such groups did eventually achieve upward social mobility, although in many cases their economic and social profiles have preserved certain distinct features.[28] There can be no doubt that race (defined in terms of skin colour and physical appearance) has remained the main marker of discrimination and disadvantage in the USA. It is probably too early to say whether this will hold true for non-European groups among recent immigrants. The evidence is that attitudes towards the different groups vary considerably, as do the specific forms of incorporation into economic and social relations.

This increase in racism must be linked to the problems of maintaining ideological legitimacy for the nation-state at a time when it is demonstrably not satisfying large sections of the population. In the period of economic expansion, social inequality could be partially masked by the fact that working-class living standards were improving. Real wages grew steadily and social insurance systems provided more security than the working class had ever known. Economic growth provided the leeway for policies of class co-operation, based on Keynesian economic ideas. Having a small slice of the cake is not so bad, when that cake is getting bigger all the time. But since the early 1970s, that situation has changed. The social and economic conditions in the old industrial areas have become extremely difficult. That is not a problem for the trans-nationals, but it is for medium-sized corporations and for the state. The political and social relations of advanced industrial societies are still significantly centred on the nation state, even if the dominant economic relations no longer are. Economic turn-around in Western Europe, North America and Australia depends, so we are told, on the cutting of real wages and the roll-back of the social security system. Moreover, this is taking place at a time of increasing social deprivation, as politics of full employment have had to be abandoned.

The neo-conservative governments which have taken on the task of social reconstruction — the Reagan Administration in the USA, Thatcher in Britain, the CDU-CSU-FDP coalition in West Germany, the Centre-Right Government in France, the Hawke-Keating Government in Australia — have had to provide ideological legitimacy for high unemployment, declining real wages, and cut-backs in welfare. This involves a new mode for the definition of the relationship between state, economy and society. Their 'authoritarian-populist discourse'[29] is based on traditional conservative values: the family, individual achievement and national identity. The causes of the social and economic crisis are identified as people who wish to sponge off social security rather than work, bureaucratic structures which stifle initiative, powerful unions which defend group privileges and restrictive practices, alien influences which threaten national unity and international terrorism.

The New Right can thus simultaneously raise the libertarian demand for 'less state' — meaning de-regulation of the economy and cuts in welfare expenditure — and demand a stronger state in terms of armed forces and policing, control of unions and restriction of civil liberties. The outside enemy — the 'Argies' in the Falklands, Gaddafi and Khomeini, the international communist conspiracy — are joined by the 'enemy within'[30]: black militants, Islamic fundamentalists, alien communist agitators who threaten law and order. On this basis, Reagan can define his policies as a crusade against 'sin and evil' and see the crisis not in terms of deep structural readjustments, but as a spiritual one, 'a test of moral will and faith'.[31] Similarly, when the Christian Democrats came to power in West Germany in 1982, they announced their intention of achieving a 'spiritual-moral turnabout'.[32]

New Right ideologies affect both immigration policies and attitudes towards existing minorities. In Western Europe there has been a general trend towards restriction of new entries, affecting migrant workers and family reunion and refugees as well. In several countries the Right has called for policies of repatriation, although this has been carried out only in a limited way in France and West Germany. Regulations on residence and labour permits have been tightened up, and powers of deportation have been extended. By making continued residence dependent on conformity to social, economic and cultural norms, such regulations help maintain a docile and flexible labour force. The USA, Canada and Australia, on the other hand, have not curtailed immigration drastically.

With regard to existing minorities, New Right policies in various countries appear to be converging. In West Germany, the emphasis until recently has been on controlling migrants through exclusion from citizenship and civil rights. They have been officially regarded as temporary workers, with no right to settle, nor to move out of wage labour by setting up businesses. Currently, the trend is, slowly and reluctantly, to recognize the reality of settlement and to allow the development of ethnic middle classes, who can be involved in strategies of social control over workers and youth. This follows the precedent of attempts to encourage 'black business' and to foster a black middle class in the USA after the riots of the 1960s. Similarly in Britain, one response to the riots of 1981 and 1985 has been the establishment of an Ethnic Enterprise Unit in the Department of Employment.[33] Big companies, such as British American Tobacco, help to sponsor small business centres in black areas, offering starting capital, management expertise and security services.

The encouragement of ethnic middle classes has a two-fold role in state strategies of conflict management. First, it helps to provide legitimacy for the system, and to prove that there are no structural barriers for racial and ethnic minorities. Writers like Thomas Sowell, a black economist and follower of Milton Friedman, have made much of the apparent economic and educational success of certain ethnic groups in the USA, particularly the Jews and Chinese, and, most recently, the Koreans.[34] The argument is that if some can make it, those who do not must suffer from some individual inadequacy or cultural disability. This is linked to the explanation of the riots of the 1960s as a result of the 'pathology of the black family'.[35] Success or failure is then not the result of class barriers or racism, but an issue of personal or cultural characteristics. These arguments have also been used to attack affirmative action programmes as an instrument for overcoming disadvantage. The argument is that such measures distort the operation of free markets, reduce the efficiency of the economy and harm everybody in the long run.

Second, the encouragement of ethnic middle classes is part of the attempt to define conflicts in terms of culture, rather than as the result of socio-economic factors and racism. In Britain, the urban unrest of the early 1980s has been officially analysed in terms of cultural difference and cultural conflict — between black and white working class youth, but also between different Afro-Carribean and Asian groups. The whole thrust is to ignore the economic causes of unrest (the high rates of unemployment and urban decline) and the political causes (heavy policing and social control through the welfare bureaucracy) and instead to emphasize social-psychological factors. Following the *Scarman Report* on the Brixton riots,[36] the official emphasis has been on ethnic groups, rather than race. In addition to encouraging ethnic business, the state has attempted to co-opt black leaders by bringing them into welfare and educational bureaucracies.

To sum up, the New Right is everywhere moving in the same direction. Their model for coping with the crisis includes a group of strategies concerning migrants and minorities which mesh in with each other, although they may appear at first sight contradictory:

- The reassertion of national values, which includes drawing ethnic boundaries to define the nation in an exclusionary (and often racist) way.
- Emphasis on free enterprise values, and rejection of state intervention to combat disadvantage. Success is attributed to 'ethnic motivation' and 'strong family values', while failure is blamed on individual inadequacy or on group pathology.
- The discovery of ethnicity as a form of social mobilization and identification, and an alternative to recognizing barriers of class, gender and racism. This is linked with analysis of conflict in culturalist terms, and encouragement of middle class ethnic leaderships as a form of social control.

What of Australia? In certain respects, Australia (and Canada too, though we shall not deal with that country here) appears to be an exception. The political economy of labour migration, both in boom and crisis, has many parallels with other countries. But the utilization of racism in state strategies of crisis management has not played a major role here. Attempts have been made to move in this direction — most notably around the 'Blainey Debate' of 1984 — but they have not had much success. Why is this?

In Chapter Seven we will examine the constraint put on state racism by the particular forms of migration and settlement developed in Australia. We will argue that multiculturalism emerged as a necessary ideology for integrating a multi-ethnic nation, and that — for all its contradictions and weaknesses — multicultural policies made a return to racism difficult and counter-productive for those in power. But we will also show how the New Right is developing new forms of racism, under a cloak of free enterprise values — sometimes even in the guise of a celebration of cultural diversity.

Notes

1. This chapter concentrates on the 'old industrial countries': Western Europe, the USA, Canada and Australia. It does not deal with the increasingly significant labour migration to oil countries, and to the 'new industrial countries' of Asia and Latin America.
2. The word 'navvies' is derived from 'navigators' and refers to the role of

the Irish in digging the canals which were crucial to British industrialization.

3. The theory of the industrial reserve army has given rise to much controversy, when applied to contemporary labour migration. There is no space for a detailed discussion of the issue here. See: Stephen Castles and Godula Kosack, *Immigrant Workers and Class Structure in Western Europe*, London: Oxford University Press 1973 and 1985, Chapter 9; S. Castles, *Here for Good — Western Europe's New Ethnic Minorities*, London: Pluto Press 1984, Chapter 2; Castles and Kosack, 'The function of labour immigration in Western European capitalism', in: *New Left Review*, No.73, July 1972; R. Miles, 'Labour migration, racism and capital accumulation', in: *Capital and Class*, 28 Spring 1986; C. Lever-Tracy, *The Segmentation and Articulation of the Working Class: An Exploration of the Impact of Post-War Australian Immigration*, PhD. Thesis, Adelaide: Flinders University 1985.

4. K. Dohse, *Auslandische Arbeiter und bürgerliche Staat,* Hain: Konigstein 1981.

5. F. Engels, 'The English elections', in: Marx and Engels, *On Britain*, Moscow: Foreign Languages Publishing House 1962; and Castles and Kosack, 'The function of labour immigration in Western European capitalism'.

6. S. Castles, *Here for Good*, 1984; S. Castles, 'The European guestworker — an obituary', in: *International Migration Review*, Vol.20 No.76, Winter 1986.

7. Department of Immigration and Ethnic Affairs, *Consolidated Statistics*, No.13, Canberra: AGPS 1982.

8. Castles, *Here for Good*, p.87.

9. OECD, *Continuous Reporting System on Migration* (SOPEMI) 1985, Paris: OECD 1986; and United Nations Economic and Social Council, *Concise Report on Monitoring of Population Trends*, New York: United Nations 1978.

10. See A. Pinkney, *The Myth of Black Progress*, Cambridge University Press 1984.

11. A. Kessler-Harris and V. Yans-McLaughlin, 'European immigrant groups', in: T. Sowell, (ed.), *American Ethnic Groups*, New York: The Urban Institute 1978.

12. US Bureau of the Census, *Statistical Abstract of the United States, 1985*, Washington D.C.: USGOP 1984.

13. *Immigration Statistics Canada* and *Canada Yearbook*, various years.

14. Department of Immigration and Ethnic Affairs, *Discussion Paper, 1986-87*, Canberra: DIEA 1986.

15. F. Fröbel, J. Heinrichs and O. Kreye, *The New International Division of Labour*, Cambridge University Press 1980.

16. S. Sassen-Koob, 'Capital mobility and labour migration: their expression in core cities', in: M.Cross (ed.), *Racial Minorities and Industrial Change*, Cambridge Univesity Press 1987.

17. See Castles, *Here for Good*, Chapter 5.

18. For W. Europe, see: OECD, *Migrants' Children and Employment: The European Experience*, Paris: OECD 1983; For Australia, see: Australian Institute of Multicultural Affairs, *Reducing the Risk — Unemployed Migrant Youth and Labour Market Programs*,

Melbourne: AIMA 1985.
19. See R. Miles, 'Labour Migration . . .', 1986.
20. Castles and Kosack, *Immigrant Workers and Class Structure in Western Europe*, Chapter 10.
21. Castles *Here for Good*, Chapter 7: R. Miles and A. Phizacklea, *White Man's Country*, London: Pluto Press 1984.
22. Castles, *Here for Good*, p.209.
23. S. Castles, 'The guests who stayed — the debate on 'Foreigners Policy' in the German Federal Republic', in: *International Migration Review*, Vol.19, No.3, Fall 1985.
24. See M. Barker *The New Racism*, London: Junction Books 1981; and Centre for Contemporary Cultural Studies, *The Empire Strikes Back*, London: Hutchinson 1982.
25. Pinkney, p.2.
26. Pinkney, p.66.
27. Pinkney, pp.78-80.
28. See Kessler-Harris and Yans-McLaughlin.
29. J. Esser and J. Hirsch 'Ein poliitsches Regulierungsmodell für den 'nachfordistischen' Kapitalismus', in: *Prokla*, No.56, September 1984.
30. Centre for Contemporary Cultural Studies, p.23.
31. Walter Stafford, in: Pinkney, p.36.
32. Castles, 'Migrants and minorities in post-Keynesian capitalism: the West German case', in: M. Cross, (ed.), *Racial Minorities and Industrial Change*, Cambridge University Press 1987.
33. A. Jakubowicz, 'Ethnicity, multiculturalism and neo-conservatism', in: G. Bottomley and M. de Lepervanche (eds), *Ethnicity, Class and Gender in Australia.*
34. T. Sowell, *Markets and Minorities*, New York: Basic Books 1981.
35. D. Moynihan, *The Negro Family: The Case for National Action*, Washington D.C.: Government Printing Office 1965.
36. Lord Scarman, *The Scarman Report — The Brixton Discorders 10-12 April 1981*, Harmondsworth: Penguin 1982.

6.
Racism, Nationalism and Australian Identity

What is 'Australian identity' in the late 1980s? Is there an 'Australian nationalism'? What ideologies and racist practices have constituted Australian identity in the past? What is the nature and impact of racism today? There are no simple answers to these questions. Possible meanings of Australian identity must be seen in the context of a rapidly changing society. Moreover, these meanings are fluid and contested in a way they have never been before. The angst-ridden and contradictory nature of the Bicentennial celebrations is evidence enough of that.

It is with the problem of the Bicentenary that this chapter will begin. In a sense, this raises in all its subtlety and complexity a wide range of questions relating to Australian identity. The chapter will then discuss the meanings of nationalism and racism. Applying these concepts to the Australian situation, we go on to discuss the ideologies of British colonialism and the post-Second World War nationalism embodied in the concept of assimilation. In Chapter Seven we will go on to analyse the replacement of this by multiculturalism and, finally, the response of the so-called New Right to the ambiguities of the current multicultural orthodoxy.

The problem of unitary national identity

Time began publishing an Australian edition in mid-1986. The lead article for its first issue was entitled 'Our Elusive Soul'. Symptomatically, the article began with a description of a naturalization ceremony in which people of different nationalities accept Australian citizenship. At the end,

> they will leave, after a supper of tea, cakes and sandwiches, and go forth into a country of neat nature strips and confused national identity. Just as the different accents merge into an indecipherable whole as eleven voices repeat the oath, Australia today is a cultural casserole, a mixture of nationalities joined more by geography than ideology. In a year of consensus, a time

of self-examination, and two years before the Bicentennial, a time of self-congratulation, we are a people unsure not only where we are going but also who we are.[1]

Mass immigration works against ideas of national unity. In Australia it has become a key motif of a process that spells the end of traditional forms of nationalism.

Talking about his Crocodile Dundee character, Hogan has said: What are we going to do, put a nice sensible hard-working accountant in a film and say 'Here's a typical Australian, hard-working, industrious'? But in 1986, the urban accountant would be much closer than a larger-than-life bushman to being the typical Australian. And he would very likely be Greek or Vietnamese — or a woman.[2]

Women, and Aborigines, as well as migrants from many different places, all challenge attempted national singularity. The dilemma of the Bicentennial was broached thus in an article in the *Sydney Morning Herald*:

So the Bicentenary is in trouble. The people running it have been blamed. Could it be that the central theme we are supposed to be celebrating, 'a sense of nationhood' or 'national identity', simply doesn't exist?

. . . What precisely is this 'Australian-ness' we are supposed to be celebrating? What generalization could you possibly make that applies to the 15 million people who live on this continent? Or even most of them?

. . . What about the 50 per cent of Australians who are women? Or the 20 per cent who are kids?

. . . What about the one in four people who come here from another country? Multicultural may be a vogue word but it describes a social reality which includes Aboriginals, Vietnamese refugees, surfies, Oxford Street homosexuals, Martin Place bankers, dole queue kids out west . . . , they are all Australians.

You can see what professional operators like David Armstrong and John Reid and even Bob Hawke are up against. Here they are trying to construct some fanciful but well-meaning sense of nationhood for us all to celebrate in 1988, and around them some 15 million people are pursuing 15 million different lives and lifestyles and not giving a damn about the attempt to turn them into Aussies instead of individuals.[3]

In the late industrial societies of the First World, the unitary ideology of nationalism becomes increasingly hard to sustain. This is particularly true for Australia which, for reasons peculiar to its own history, has never had a strong nationalism. The disintegration of a unitary ideology of the nation is epitomized in the move from official state policies of assimilation of culturally different 'others' (the Aborigines and immigrants) to a multiculturalism which respects their differences. This is where the Bicentennial, ostensibly celebrating the moment of English colonial settlement and the emergence of a single nation, becomes a very contradictory exercise. To build up this argument here and in the following chapter, we first need, however, to define the key concepts of nationalism and racism.

Nationalism

Nationalism is an ideology of social unity, 'imagined community' as Benedict Anderson calls it, which describes a so-called 'people' who live within the boundaries of a nation-state. Both nation-states and the ideology of nationalism, according to Anderson and the other major recent theorist of nationalism, Ernest Gellner, are modern phenomena. Gellner points out that communities in agricultural societies were localized and relatively insulated laterally. Not only did popular language and folk culture vary considerably from place to place, but the ruling class operated with ancient and sacred languages whose boundaries extended much farther than modern states. The state, such that it was, extracted taxes and maintained the peace but had little or no interest in promoting communication between its subject communities.[4]

Adopting Weber's notion of the state as 'that agency within society which possesses the monopoly of legitimate violence', Gellner goes on to argue about the peculiar nature of industrialism with its massive and complex division of labour, the need for a sophisticated regulatory apparatus, and the necessary mobility of its workforce. This means that the degree of popular cultural-linguistic diversity characteristic of agrarian society is no longer possible. The state has to universalize one language for principal currency in everyday life. Despite considerable work specialization, the linguistic-cultural distance between specialists is not great. 'Their mysteries are far closer to mutual intelligibility, their manuals have idioms which overlap to a much greater extent and retraining, though sometimes difficult, is not generally an awesome task.'[5]

Nationalism, then, is 'the organization of human groups into large, centrally educated, culturally homogeneous units', co-terminous with the nation-state.[6] This is a new phenomenon, historically specific and necessary to industrialism. The pivotal instrument of its cultural creation and reproduction, according to Gellner, is the state-run education system. Ending the radical linguistic-cultural disjunction of high and folk cultures, the modern education system teaches towards literacy in a single national language, a function necessary in a society 'in which its members are and must be mobile, and ready to shift from one activity to another . . .' Moreover, 'in the course of their work they must constantly communicate with a large number of other men, with whom they frequently have no previous association, and with whom communication must consequently be explicit, rather than relying on context.' No longer can socialization be left up to the particularities of local kin-culture.

> Exo-socialization, the production and reproduction of men outside the local intimate unit is now the norm, and must be so. The imperative exo-socialization is the main clue to why the state and culture *must* now be linked, whereas in the past their connection was thin, fortuitous, varied, loose, and often minimal.[7]

Anderson also sees socio-linguistic developments as critically indicative of significant historical change. With the rise of 'print capitalism', mass producing books in the newly constructed written forms of vernacular languages, Anderson notes changes in forms of consciousness. For example, within these new territorial, vernacular print languages, new forms of temporality, as elements of a new and necessarily imagined form of community, emerge. 'An American will never meet, or even know the names of more than a handful of his 240,000,000-odd fellow-Americans.' He has no idea of precisely what his compatriots are doing at any one moment. But through, for example, the narratives of the news and the knowledge of massive simultaneous readership, 'he has complete confidence in their steady, anonymous, simultaneous activity.'[8]

Nationalism becomes a crucial feature in the cultural construction and ideological legitimation of the new nation-states of industrialism. Seton-Watson distinguishes a nation as 'a community of people, whose members are bound together by a sense of solidarity, a common culture, a national consciousness', from a state as 'a legal and political organization with the power to require obedience and loyalty from its citizens.' Nationalism, as a political movement, has generally sought one or both of two things, 'independence (the creation of a sovereign state in which the nation is dominant), and national unity (the incorporation within the frontiers of this state of all groups which are considered, by themselves, or by those who claim to speak for them, to belong to the nation)'.[9] The process of the establishment and legitimation of nation-states through nationalism by no means follows an uncomplicated or peaceful course. In an argument directly parallel to Seton-Watson's, Gellner points to two major historical processes through which nationalism attempts to construct 'cultural homogeneity': through struggle for the establishment of new nation-states or through assimilation to the cultural pool of an established nation-state. But this is not merely a cultural construction. 'It is not the case that nationalism imposes homogeneity out of wilful cultural *Machtbedrüfniss*; (it is) the objective need for homogeneity which is reflected in nationalism.'[10]

Even if the general phenomenon of nationalism is firmly grounded in the history of industrial society, its content, nevertheless, is ideological. Nations, despite their own pretensions to primordiality, are far from original or natural.

The cultural shreds and patches used by nationalism are often arbitrary historical inventions. But in no way does it follow that the principle of nationalism itself, as opposed to the avatars it happens to pick up for its incarnations, is itself in the least contingent and accidental.

As Gellner goes on to argue, nationalism 'conquers in the name of a putative folk culture'. In fact, it involves the 'generalized diffusion of a school-mediated, academy-supervised idiom, codified for the requirements of reasonably precise bureaucratic and technological communication', and the 'establishment of an anonymous, impersonal society, with mutually substitutable atomized individuals'.[11] It is the discrepancy between the pretensions of the nationalist story line and its real historical function that makes it ideological.

Anderson characterizes the ideology of the community of nationalism by the style of its imagining. 'Regardless of the actual inequality and exploitation that may prevail — in each, the nation is always conceived as a deep, horizontal comradeship.' In practical terms, nationalism constructs a secularized immortality, which finds its emblem in death in war. People, he points out, will die for the nation because it is ostensibly immortal, in a way that they would not die, say, for liberalism.[12] Nationalism is a new ideology of a transcendent power above the individual, however earthly its actual ends and effects.

The foregoing brief discussion of some significant aspects of the literature on nationalism will serve as a framework for identifying and interpreting the old Australian nationalism. But it is by no means the whole of our analysis. In fact, our main interest is the nature of the move to a new, multicultural reading of plural Australian identities. Our central thesis is that in the late industrialism of the First World, traditional nationalisms no longer hold. New forms of communal identity are emerging, albeit contradictory and conflict-ridden, which constitute new pluralist umbrellas to legitimate the boundaries of the state. Perhaps one might like to call these nationalisms (celebrating a nation's 'multiculturalism', for example), although that is a purely semantic question and seemingly a contradiction in terms. Our interest is the substance of the move, in which the old ideology of nationalism no longer makes the sense it once did; as it becomes less and less possible and necessary to identify and maintain a singular national 'folk'; and as old forms of racism prove themselves less able to mobilize populations. But, before developing these arguments, we must try to identify the peculiar conditions of late industrial culture which form their basis.

Cultural theorist and historian Frederic Jameson divides the history of industrial society into three major phases: market capitalism, monopoly or imperialist capitalism and the era of multinational or consumer capitalism. This last phase is characterized not by the relatively straightforward imperialist extension of the commodity form of an earlier phase, but the expansion of capital into previously un-commodified areas, a new and historically original penetration and colonization of nature and the unconscious; that is, the destruction of pre-industrial Third World agriculture by the Green Revolution, and the rise of the media and the 'advertising industry'.[13] To these extensive internal colonizations of nature and culture, we must add significant changes in the domestic realm as more women become involved in wage-work and many domestic products and services become commodities and are subject to technological change. In terms of political-economic structures, and in the manufactured culture of this new phase of world industrial development, unprecedented internationalization reduces the importance that the nation-state had in the imperialism/monopoly phase. Crucial new developments include the emergence of trans-national industrial and finance corporations which now dominate both capitalist and 'actually existing socialist' societies, the striking uniformity of the whole-world market of consumer goods, and the internationalization of media networks and mass culture.

Do these trends towards economic and cultural universalism lead to a withering away of the nation-state? Such predictions have been made both in the liberal-modernist and the socialist camp. Yet the twentieth century has been, and still is, plagued by bloody wars and conflicts fought among nation-states and nationalist movements. The most advanced countries of Europe are still disrupted by ethnic-based national liberation movements — Basques in Spain, Irish Catholics in Britain, Bretons and Corsicans in France. 'Glasnost' in the Soviet Union has released suppressed national conflicts; now the Tartars and Ukranians, the Latvians, Estonians and Letts dare to demand independence. However, in the New World states, which have uncontested borders and no serious separatist movements, the decline of nationalism is most evident. Perhaps, we might argue, Australia is unusually advanced along the post-nationalist path, having had a relatively weak nationalism to reconstruct.

Yet, rather ironically, the same historical processes which lead to a certain level of world economic and cultural integration also throw differences together in an unprecedented cultural-linguistic tower of Babel: labour migrants with traits developed in different parts of the globe; mundane commodities from exotic-sounding places and exotic commodities produced in mundane factories; languages, discourses within languages, and genres within discourses; varieties of sexuality and domestic relationship. This, too, is very much the case for late twentieth century Australia.

Racism

Nationalism, founded so strongly as it is on an ideology of kinship, frequently takes the form of racism in ascribing causal significance and moral superiority to visible manifestations of tradition and physical or phenotypical peculiarity. As Nairn argues, it is the ideological character of nationalism that has produced the most fertile ground for modern irrationalisms, principally racism.[14] Confident nationalisms often include racist expressions of superiority, a definition of our particular virtue, the differentiation of 'us' from an inferior 'them'.

In commonsense parlance, 'race' refers only to phenotypes (visible physical differences) and only to certain phenotypes at that. Variations in height (which occur as much within as between 'races') are obviously not considered so significant in determining 'race' as differences in skin colour, for example. There are many other types of human physiological variation whose archaic geographical boundaries do not coincide with those of skin-colour, such as blood-types and immune systems. Furthermore, the reality of the archaic world physiological map is more one of continuous variation than distinct 'racial' boundaries. Indeed, average genetic variation between populations has been shown to be nowhere near as significant as genetic variation within populations. Finally, in biological terms, differences between human groups are very minor, and, in generational terms, very recent.[15]

As races do not exist in nature, the commonsense etymology of the term 'racism' is deceptive. Racism is an ideology which gives causal social and historical significance to appearances of biological difference. It is a cultural construction, rather than a biologically based phenomenon, extrapolating from visible differences into supposedly fixed cultural and historical attributes. Racism is a demonstrable misconception, a handy rationalization and naturalization of certain social actions and relations of inequality. This definition should not be taken to mean that racism is simply an illusion or a malicious fiction. We have discussed the sociological and historical realities of structural racism in the Australian and international context in other chapters of this book.

Racism and colonialism

We will now, in this and the following chapter, attempt to apply the concepts of nationalism and racism to an understanding of developments in Australian identity. To do this we will take four important moments in Australian identity: the logic of British colonialism of the eighteenth and nineteenth centuries, the post-Second World War ideology of assimilation; the policy of multiculturalism and, finally, the present rumblings of the so-called 'New Right'. Our purpose is to examine significant moments in Australian identity which reflect key historical processes at different points in Australian history. This by no means exhausts the range and complex inter-relations of various cultural and social identifications across Australian history.

Philosopher David Hume set the ideological tone of English colonialism very clearly:

I am apt to suspect the negroes and in general all the other species of men . . . to be naturally inferior to the whites. There never was a civilized nation of any other complexion than white, nor even any individual eminent either in action or speculation . . . Such a uniform and constant difference could not happen, in so many countries and ages, if nature had not made an original distinction betwixt these breeds of men.[16]

Different social relations have frequently been seen to correlate with phenotypical variations. This has been the basis of classical biologically-based racism. So, Aboriginal peoples have seemed more natural and less human than those whose farming, housing and technologies appeared as the fullest expression of humanity. William Charles Wentworth, the famous nineteenth-century Australian landowner and politician, writing in 1819 employed the classical device of reducing an historical cultural judgment to an assertion of biological superiority:

The Aborigines of this country occupy the lowest place in the gradatory scale of the human species. They have neither houses nor clothing; they are entirely unacquainted with the arts of agriculture; and even (their arms and implements) are of the rudest contrivance and workmanship. Thirty years' intercourse with Europeans has not effected the slightest change in their habits; and even those who have most intermixed with the colonists have never been prevailed upon to practise one of the arts of civilized life.[17]

Not only is the linking of supposed Aboriginal cultural inferiority with biological inferiority (a fixed place on 'the gradatory scale of the human species') a fallacy, but the cultural assessment, too, is a fallacy. There is simply no truth to the view that the Aborigines were without profound and complex human-technological relations with nature: using, shaping and scientifically analyzing nature. With their own historical blinkers, wanting to project their own history as the most fully human, those shifting the frontiers of industrialism mistook the Aboriginal peoples. This was not simply in error, but part of a process of rationalizing genocide and the theft of land. To give two concrete examples, when Blaxland, Wentworth and Lawson crossed the Blue Mountains to the west of Sydney in 1813, they were elated to find extensive grazing lands. But this idea of the bountiful potential of this 'wilderness' was based on a cultural misapprehension. In fact, what they saw was far from 'natural' or 'wilderness'. It was a human construction. Aborigines had profoundly shaped the Australian environment to suit their own ecological needs, systematically clearing the land with fire. Furthermore, the European 'explorers' and settlers used the Aborigines' well-trodden routes.

Similarly, nineteenth-century settlers in the Pilaga in North-West New South Wales found what appeared to them to be a wilderness ideally suited to grazing. Against Aboriginal resistance, they fenced and built houses. But within several decades, the scrub that the Aborigines had kept cleared for tens of thousands of years had grown back. The original European settlement lost its viability and was abandoned.

The ideology of English colonial settlement was simply unable to see Aboriginal culture and the significance of its shaping of nature. This cultural 'invisibility' was clearly very convenient for the European 'explorers' and settlers. Critical in the chain of rationalizations, however, was the racist connection of supposed cultural inferiority with natural inferiority.

Although different social relations in nature are at the bottom of arguments about superiority and 'true' humanity, in the classical racism of colonialism this historical variation is enshrined as biological, genetic and permanent. The historical variation and rationalization of the harm done by one group to another is put down to what are supposed to be 'natural' human variations. For 'social Darwinism', human history was only further proof of the general theory; it was a process of the 'natural' selection of genetically superior races. The imperialists had every right to conquer. It was the 'natural' outcome of their genetic superiority, their mission in 'natural' history. These characteristic features of classical racism are very clearly in evidence in the quotations from Hume and Wentworth, above, and in the active historical process of European settlement in Australia, against Aboriginal resistance.

Assimilation and nationalism

In the post-Second World War years, there emerged an official policy of cultural assimilation for immigrants and Aborigines. We have already given an historical account of these developments in Chapter Three. Our purpose now is to analyze this moment in Australian identity in terms of the key concepts of nationalism and racism.

This discussion needs to be prefaced, however, with the observation that British colonialism was racist, but not nationalist in any of the modern senses of that term. First, and most obviously, Australia was not a nation in the eighteenth and nineteenth centuries, but a number of separate English colonies. Second, the ideology of the state was not nationalist (drawing imagined kin-identity as co-terminous with the boundaries of the state), but clearly colonial, harking back to the culture of the mother country and the authority of the imperial monarch. Third, no attempts were made to include 'others' culturally (such as the Aborigines and the Irish) as is the classical assimilative, unificatory project of the emerging nation-state.

In terms of dominant forms of identity and official state policy, the assimilation of the post-1945 decades, we would like to argue provocatively, is the first historically significant nationalism in Australian history. It is a nationalism with enduring racist elements, but nevertheless clearly distinguishable from the racism of English colonialism.

In a passage symbolic of the historical and social vision of the era, Russel Ward wrote in a junior secondary history textbook first published in 1952,

> There are still living today in Arnhem Land people who know almost no history. They are Aboriginal tribesmen who live in practically the same way as their forefathers and ours did, tens of thousands of years ago. Like them they have not only no accurate knowledge of past events, but no aeroplanes, motor-cars or picture shows; not even any books, houses or clothes. Apart from the fact that they use weapons of stone and wood to hunt for their food, their lives are almost as hard and dangerous as those of the animals, who also hunt to live. We are civilized today and they are not. History helps us to understand why this is so.
>
> This is not because the Arnhem-landers are more stupid than we are. Scientists have proved that there is very little difference, on the average, between the natural, inborn cleverness or intelligence of different peoples; but there are very great differences in their knowledge — in what they know, or have learnt from other races.[18]

This represents an important shift away from the biological analysis of classical racism. Unlike W.C. Wentworth, nearly a century and a half before, the Aborigines, for Ward, are redeemable. 'Our' superiority is historical and cultural, not biological. Aborigines, to paraphrase the rest of Ward's 1952 textbook conception of history, were remnants of 'Early Man' to be located at one end of a series of 'ages' in the relentless self-improvement of 'Man' as 'he' evolves steadily away from 'his' animal ancestors and becomes more and more human. Symptomatic of this historical framework of condemnation of gathering and hunting is a negative terminology of primitivism in which Aborigines are 'wandering savages', 'tribesmen', and 'natives'. In this negative definition, gathering-hunting culture is depicted as a series of absences, principally of modern cultural artefacts. History is conceived as progress, using a teleology which culminates in the technological triumphs of industrialism. A qualitative break in this historical evolution was the development of civilization (settlement, agriculture, urbanism) which began fully human history. Aborigines had no civilization and thus no history. They had been dominated by nature, isolated from progress and had made no progress on their own. As a corollary, the 'Modern World', triumphing in industrialism, is characterized as the active making of history, and the mastery of nature. Industrialism, as the purpose or end of history, is to be eulogized for its technical artefacts, for its knowledge and for its ability to dominate nature.[19]

The term 'race' is still used in this analysis, but not as a biological category. Rather, races are equated with civilization or non-civilization. This historical-cultural conception of superiority, then, does not condemn 'others' to immutable inferiority by virtue of evolutionary laws of nature. Rather, it condemns by means of evolutionary laws of history. As an evolution which is historical, the differences of 'race' are not irretrievable. There is hope for 'them'. They can learn to be like 'us' and share in 'our' progress. Indeed, it is our duty to see that this happens. Hence the paradigm of assimilation as the solution to the 'problem' of cultural difference. This was the consensus view of both right and left commentators on Australian identity and social policy makers until the late 1960s.

Precisely this paradigm is also used to interpret and remedy the 'problem' of cultural differences in immigration. The story of progress and development is a determined and singular narrative, with different 'others' choosing to join in its course, to contribute their labour and enterprise, and to reap its material benefits. To explain the particular Australian nationalism on which assimilation was premised, we need to examine the ideology of 'The Australian Way of Life' of the post-1945 decades.

If any single slogan encapsulated popular conceptions of Australian-ness from about the mid-1940s to the mid-1960s, it was 'The Australian Way of Life'. It meant, above all, high standards of living in an advanced industrial, market society. All people would receive their share of the material benefits of a revitalized culture of progress and development. This classless, populist Australian Way was defined in sharp contrast to communism or poverty, both found in abundance in Asia. A suburban dreamtime of the new Australian present, an animism of consumer durables, was to be the bounty of a 'free' enterprise springing to life after the horrors of fascism and war.

The fuel for the Australian Way was industrial development, represented most dramatically by the Snowy Mountains Scheme. This project was almost the size of the Tennesee Valley Project in the United States and was undoubtedly an enormous enterprise for a country with a barely industrial infrastructure. It symbolized the peculiar nature of Australian post-war development in a number of ways. For a start, as the keystone of the material and moral endeavour of development, it received bi-partisan support. A Labor government initiated it and the Tory Menzies Government went on to see it finished, with commitment equal to their Labor opponents. It is also symptomatic that it was a state rather than a 'free' enterprise. Menzies simply continued Labor's project, one side of which involved the state integrally in major projects of economic development, right down to protecting and subsidizing 'free' enterprise throughout the economy. The other side of state intervention, also in a bi-partisan progression from the late-1940s, was the extension of the welfare state, from direct welfare payments through to massive expansion in public education. This course of progress was explicitly linked to the Australian Way.

Perhaps most indicative of the great engine of progress symbolized in the Snowy Mountains Scheme, however, was the role of post-war immigration in its construction. It would be built by migrants from England and refugees from Europe, willing to offer their hard labour for the promise of joining the Australian Way. Immigrants would assimilate to the benefit of themselves and Australia. Again, both Labor and Liberal parties could find nothing substantial to disagree about in this course of action. In the two post-war decades, the Australian population rose from seven and a half million to eleven million, largely due to the arrival of over two million immigrants.

Nationalism was a critical ideological tool in this period, not only to create the illusion of social unity as a pretext for the massive project of development inspired by the nation-state, but also to 'sell' the supposed assimilability of large numbers of potentially threatening 'others' to a working-class with a history of both trade unionism and racism. The Australian Way, moreover, for these few decades, seemed to live up to its promise. Standards of living for ordinary people were almost constantly improving and many immigrants achieved their hopes in material assimilation to suburbia's desires. Nor did these immigrants lower the living standards of the existing working-class. In fact, they took the worst paid and least pleasant jobs. Longstanding racist and union fears, in the context of boom-time, proved to be unfounded, even if assimilation was in reality a front for segmentation and structural racism. The state even set about fixing the Aboriginal problem once and for all, also through assimilation, in this special case in the form of welfare paternalism.

The Australian Way of Life was the practical vindication for ordinary people of industrial progress and development. Even the great labour historians run this nationalist line. For Gollan, the essence of Australian history is the search to 'make life more tolerable for the majority of the people', while Fitzpatrick writes explicitly of the development of the industrial and urban 'Australian Way of Life'. After all,

> Australians are high, in world comparisons, as telephone users, car owners, radio listeners, parties to marriage ceremonies, and exponents of competitive sports and games . . . . It is a feature of Australian life that the vast majority of people prefer to live, and are able to live, in one-family homes with front and back gardens . . . The Australian people made heroes of none, and raised no

idols, except perhaps an outlaw, Ned Kelly and Carbine, a horse. But, generation after generation, they fought with beasts at Ephesus — blight and drought, fire and flood; their own taskmasters and the covetous alien — and, suffering their setbacks, still made of Australia a home good enough for men of modest report to live in, calling their souls their own.[20]

A populist culture of middle Australian-ness became the other side of the coin of high standards of living. The immigrants who came from different countries, came to fit into this Australian Way of Life.

New Australians, amounting to a ninth of the whole Australian population by 1956, were settling down to try to understand, if not share, old Australian predilections for drinking tea, rather than coffee, beer rather than the good wine of the country; in the south-east, south and west of the continent playing Australian-rules, rather than soccer or Rugby football (the chief winter game in New South Wales and Queensland only). Newcomers had to puzzle over the old Australian disrespect for civil order and good government, bewilderingly joined with a general observance of the peace . . . And, new Australians had to try to understand old Australian speech.[21]

This singularity of Australian-ness, encapsulated in the Australian Way, was a type of nationalism, crucial for a state newly and massively implicated in development and immigration. In essence, both left and right variants of the story were in agreement on the substance of this cultural 'reality'. Critical elements in imagining community for the project of development were the erasure of differences in gender role through the archetypically male imagery and the active construction of policies of assimilation for Aborigines and immigrant others. Admittedly this nationalism does not have the 'folk' connotations of many others — that is, the roots in imagined common experience and traditions. But its project of imagining continuous community for the purpose of development, together with its racist demand that immigrants must assimilate to a community considered superior, make up an ideology which is, both in form and function, a nationalism.

Even though the expropriation of the lands of gatherers and hunters and the process of mass immigration are historical events which are hardly comparable in any way, it is more than coincidental that the same idea of assimilation and the same public policy should have been used to conceive and 'remedy' cultural difference. Nor, as we will argue in the next chapter, is it coincidental that assimilation should be replaced with multiculturalism in the area of immigration and ethnic affairs at the same moment that a cultural pluralism advocating autonomous Aboriginality replaced assimilation as a policy for Aborigines.

To sum up, assimilation was an ideology of unitariness which in many important ways took the form of a classical nationalism.

Taking the project of post-war economic reconstruction and mass immigration together, assimilation set out to construct cultural homogeneity for the purpose of national development.

As much as it is an instance of the general phenomenon, however, it seems to rely less on the language of kin and the ideology of folk than is commonly the case for nationalisms, principally because of the ambiguities and tensions of the English-imperial connection and independent Australian nationalism. In the case of the former, the colonial link was a less than plausible basis for an identity that would purport to capture the essence of the people who lived within the boundaries of the Australian nation-state. And, in the case of the latter, no claims to peculiarly local folk primordiality were possible for the European settlers. Pre-eminently, instead, the language of nationalism, celebrating the imagined communal 'us', was about standards of living and domestic progress. This is an unusually 'modern' celebration for nationalism, perhaps, but, linked neverthe-less with an explicit ideal of cultural assimilation. The traditional function of a nationalism is thus clearly being performed, right down to the racist contradistinctions of 'us' from unacceptable cultural 'others', such as the material threat of the 'yellow peril'.

By the late 1970s, however, this fledgling Australian nationalism was beginning to come apart. Symptomatic of the change was the replacement of the official policy assimilation or integration with one of cultural pluralism. Deeper down, the nation-state was begin-ning to lose its political and cultural significance, as culture and identity increasingly took on stronger international and local or sub-cultural dimensions. We will continue this narrative of Australian identity in the next chapter by examining the multi-faceted causes of the end of singular national identity, and then describing the strident reaction of the so-called New Right who, in one way or another, ad-vocate a return to the old assimilating nationalism against what they see as the degeneracy of liberal multiculturalism.

Notes

1. A. Attwood, 'Our elusive soul', *Time Australia*, 21 July 1986, pp.48-49.
2. Attwood, p.50.
3. Tony McLellan, 'What exactly are we celebrating in 1988?', *Sydney Morning Herald*, 16 March 1986.
4. Ernest Gellner, *Nations and Nationalism*, London: Basil Blackwell 1983, pp.10-11; Benedict Anderson, *Imagined Communities: Reflec-tions on the Origins and Spread of Nationalism*, London: Verso 1983, pp.23,25,31,40.
5. Gellner, pp.24-37.
6. Gellner, p.27.
7. Gellner, p.37.
8. Anderson, pp.23-40.

9.   Hugh Seton-Watson, *Nations and States: An Enquiry into the Origins of Nations and the Politics of Nationalism*, London: Methuen 1977, pp.1-3.
10.   Gellner, pp.39,46.
11.   Gellner, p.56.
12.   Anderson, pp.16, 18-19.
13.   Frederic Jameson, 'Post-modernism, or the cultural logic of late capitalism', *New Left Review*, No.146, July-August 1984, pp.53-93.
14.   Tom Nairn, *The Break-up of Britain: Crisis and Neo-Nationalism*, London: New Left Books 1977, p.337.
15.   Bill Cope, 'Racism and naturalness', paper presented to the *Cultural Construction of Race Conference*, University of Sydney, 4-5 August, 1985, Sydney: Social Literacy Monograph Series.
16.   Quoted in A.T. Yarwood and S. Knowling, *Race Relations in Australian History*, Sydney: Methuen 1982, p.16.
17.   Quoted in Yarwood and Knowling, p.20.
18.   Russel Ward, *Man Makes History: World History from the Earliest Times to the Renaissance*, Sydney: Shakespeare Head Press 1952, p.7.
19.   See Bill Cope, 'Losing the Australian Way: The Rise of Multiculturalism and the Crisis of National Identity', Ph.D Thesis, (unpublished) Macquarie University 1987.
20.   Robin Gollan, *Radical and Working Class Politics*, Melbourne: University Press 1960, p.viii; Brian Fitzpatrick, *The Australian People, 1788-1945*, Melbourne: University Press 1951, p.255.
21.   Fitzpatrick, pp.24-25.

7.
Multiculturalism and the New Right

The decline of the Australian way of life

In this chapter we will argue that the now dominant view of Australia as a multicultural society will not sustain a nationalism able to perform its traditional ideological function. Put simply, the project of imagining communality, imagining the shared mission of the nation, imagining our domestic progress as all of us move simultaneously through history, is torn apart by a new emphasis on cultural differences. Apart from the material fact that we can no longer believe strongly in the reality of that progress, we now also imagine formally equal and culturally relative differences, of ethnicity, gender or 'lifestyle'. But a New Right looms on the ideological horizon, advocating a revival of nationalism as a way of resolving our social and economic woes.

In the same way that we opened our discussion of assimilation and nationalism with a quote from Russel Ward's school textbook, we will set the tone for our discussion of multiculturalism with two quotes from recent school curriculum materials.

Throughout its history, Australian society has always been culturally diverse. Prior to culture contact with Europeans, Aboriginal belief systems, social patterns, exchange systems and local group identity varied considerably from one environment to another. Likewise, English, Scottish, Welsh and Irish immigrants of the early colonial period varied considerably in terms of geographic origins, social class, religion, folk traditions, education and political outlook. Since 1788, the cultural diversity of Australia has been expanded. Immigration and the interaction of a wide range of Australian ethnic groups have been instrumental in the development of an Australian multicultural society.[1]

Aboriginal Studies is not to be involved in the general theme of Multicultural Studies as is presently and naively done. We, the Aboriginal people, are a unique group within Australia. We are the undisputed indigenous people of this continent. We have a distinct and separate culture from that of non-Aboriginal people. Much emphasis has been placed on the theory that we migrated to this land. There is no evidence to support this. Our history states we originated from this continent. We have always been here.[2]

Australian history is characterized here simply as differences. In the first quote it is clear that there were lots of cultures in Australia before European settlement and lots have been added since. Difference is to be celebrated and cultures are relativized or made formally equal in a nice, non-exclusionary Australian history. In the second quote, Aborigines clearly resent being lumped in as another culture among the many. Their experience has not been one in which cultural difference is a positive and colourful phenomenon. Yet the perspective of this quote, too, is cultural pluralism, even if it is a stronger version, tending towards cultural separatism. To put this cultural and ideological move in perspective, we will set an historical background to the demise of nationalism.

By the late 1960s, the hold of the old, assimilating nationalist ideology of the Australian Way was beginning to weaken. One of the roots of this was the fact that in real terms, the old Australian Way of Life was falling apart. The foundations for this decline had been laid in the previous decades: labour intensive manufacturing industry and a dependence on primary industries in export markets, to name just two key characteristics of the Australian economy. At first the problems did not seem so fundamental that they could shatter the peaceful assuredness of the suburban dreamtime. While Poseidon's nickel discovery sent its shares skyrocketing from almost nothing to $250 per share, Menzies' successors in the Liberal party were losing their grip on development. A series of weak and incompetent leaders found themselves going all the way with LBJ into disaster in Vietnam; facing the spread of a world-wide youth counter-culture into Australia; and increasingly unable to fiddle the fiscal policy of the state as they had in the past to ensure nearly full employment and low inflation.

Whitlam's Labor Government followed in 1972, with a grand programme for the extension of the welfare state and an increase in the state's role in development. Massive schemes were envisaged to 'buy back the farm', for the state to invest in mining and industry. Labor, however, was less concerned with installing ordinary people in power than to establish a programme couched in the language of nationalist modernization, so the Australian welfare state, a united Australian industrial nation, might lead the world with its material progress. Sweden and West Germany were touted as models. Labor's 1972-5 Government represents the last gasp of the post-war nationalism of the Australian Way.

As the world recession of the 1970s ripened, Labor's policies were nothing less than suicidal, more and more Keynesian as Keynesian-ism became less and less viable. Increasing fiscal crisis of the state was aggravated by increased welfare and development spending. Some real, if relatively miniscule, redistribution of wealth produced a revolt of the industrialists (who increasingly were moving their manufacturing to Asia anyway), the media barons and finally, with the 'coup' of November 1975, the middle ground of voters who felt correctly some real loss of the Australian Way.

Australia then, was genuinely to break new ground, to lead the world. A wealthy sheep farmer, who had been subsidized by his family to get his third class honours from Oxford, proceeded to administer the medicine of what was destined to be the new Western economic order. Having read Ayn Rand and Milton Friedman, Fraser began to introduce serious economic liberalism before Margaret Thatcher and Ronald Reagan had even gained government. In the new age of free enterprise, it would be obvious that life was not meant to be easy, welfare would be a matter of minimally assisted self-help and the state's role in development would be rolled back to allow the fruits of the 'natural' forces of the free market economy to bear. And, just as much as Whitlam pursued Menzies' nationalist developmentalism to its disintegration, so the Hawke Labor Government that succeeded Fraser would be more liberal in its economic policies than Fraser himself had been.

By the mid-1980s, the Australian Way has been lost. Standards of living for ordinary people are declining in real terms and the Hawke Government is telling its constituents that the present medicine for the eventual future health of the system is considerable personal restraint. Real wages will have to decrease, and the party on better terms with the labour movement is better able to cajole it into 'realism'.

Much of manufacturing industry has left for Asia. The Holden, barely retaining its name, is largely made of imported parts of General Motors' world car and is making massive annual losses, year after year. In half a decade, the Japanese Yen has gained 400 per cent in value against the Australian dollar. The bottom has fallen out of the world commodities market. Large numbers of small and mid-size Australian farmers, the most efficient in the world, are going broke and the Australian state cannot afford the massive subsidies shelled out by the European and American governments to keep their farmers above water. And many mining sectors are no longer so profitable.

But, as if all this has not been bad enough for the nationalism of the Australian Way, there have been other, fragmenting histories at work. New Left social critics started to point to the cultural and historical impoverishment of the cultural nationalism of the Australian Way even before it began to fall apart. Besotted with affluence in 'Godzone', the Australian man sits slouched and stupid amid his dreams.

A block of land, a brick veneer and a motor-mower beside him in the wilderness — what more does he want to sustain him, except a Holden to polish, a beer with the boys, marital sex on Saturday nights, a few furtive adulteries, an occasional gamble on the horses or the lottery, the tribal rituals of football, the flickering shadows in his lounge room of cops and robbers, goodies and baddies, guys and dolls.[3]

Not that an incipient New Right could not see the same thing, in the figures of Bazza and Dame Edna.

As it became increasingly obvious that Labor and Liberal policies were variations on similar themes, and vanguard parties with ideas of social structure and historical process imported from Euro-communism rose somewhat and then faded, the only active counter-cultures were fragmented into separate 'new social movements': a feminist movement, an ecology movement, a peace movement and movements advocating cultural pluralism. These have been critical elements in the erosion of nationalism.

As women's worldwide role in the employment economy, and the nature of the traditional nuclear family changed, so there emerged a powerful international women's movement. In Australia, not only was it able to demand reforms within the bureaucracies of government through the Women's Electoral Lobby and Equal Employment Opportunity, for example it was able also to form a separate politics of women's culture with which to conduct specialist social criticism.

Inspired in part by the black political movements of the United States, Aborigines came to reject assimilation. Aboriginal self-determination would not universally mean accepting the dubious merits of advanced industrial life. Aboriginality was worthy of its own high self-esteem, and a central task of the movement was the demand for Land Rights. Despite the fact that at least some of the material promise of the Australian Way of Life was realized for many immigrants, assimilation was becoming less plausible a story as the mass migration programme moved on. The migration net was cast increasingly far afield. The numbers of immigrants continued to grow, and the different faces did not simply disappear into the crowd. Cultural variety was obvious and a new range of specialist welfare issues presented themselves. There arose from the late 1960s organizations and movements constituting an ethnic politics, in full swing by the late 1970s. They demanded welfare services. They rallied around cultural differences. With the large scale arrival of Indochinese refugees in the Fraser period, discussed in Chapter Four, the cultural differences had gone well beyond those envisaged by the immigration minister who had begun it all, Arthur Calwell.

By the late 1970s, the old, nationalist, assimilating versions of Australian identity had become quaintly anachronistic. The whole frame of historical interpretation and ideological purpose had shifted. Symptomatically, cultural historian Richard White set out to prove there is 'no 'real' Australia waiting to be uncovered'. Indeed, there is no point asking whether 'one version of (the) essential Australia is truer than another because they are all intellectual constructs, neat, tidy, comprehensible and necessarily false.'[4] This appeared especially to be the case in the 1980s, with the women's movement, Aboriginal politics and multiculturalism in full flower. Together, these movements overturned the old culture of nationalism, central to which was the ideology of the Australian Way. In an immediate sense, this is a literal undermining of its story-line. But, more seriously, in our late industrial society, the conditions for the existence of an ideology of continuous cultural community have been largely removed. No longer are there any great state projects of development around which 'we' might rally. Indeed, the Australian state appears increasingly to be no more than an office for the local management of the requirements of multinational industry and finance. At the same time, late industrialism fragments into separate sub-cultures and identities. This is the result on the one hand of movements critically attempting to revise the racism or sexism of the older ideologies and practices of the nation. On the other hand, we live with the ironical historical tendency of an ever-universalizing and internationalizing world society to juxtapose cultural differences, uninterested in these differences so long as they do not challenge the dominant system of labour and consumption.

The rise of multiculturalism

Having set the context to the demise of the old, assimilating, nationalist Australian identity, what does multiculturalism mean? Chapter Four has already answered this question in terms of the history of social policy and government practice. We will now analyse critically the meaning of culture for multiculturalism, and its consequent practical limitations. To begin, we will discuss the tensions evident in the rise of 'ethnic politics' in Australia.

Ethnic politics was a phenomenon which began with the sheer weight of non-English speaking migrant numbers and their relative social disadvantage. From this base-point, it became politically complex and culturally ambiguous. The growth of organizations like the Ethnic Communities' Councils came with the social success of a small number of articulate 'community leaders', angered by what they perceived to be the barriers to social mobility for those of non-English speaking background: prejudice, unrecognized professional job qualifications, and so on. Characteristically, the perspective was one of those who saw their non-English speaking background as a hindrance to social success in Australia, despite their being political refugees to the 'free-world', despite their overseas educational qualifications or despite their expectations. So, 'ethnic politics' has often been not simply the voice of the disadvantaged majority of non-English speaking migrants, but the voice of an atypical few. And, complicating matters further, 'ethnic politics' evoked a response from government. Perhaps it was a cynical judgement about how to catch the 'migrant vote'. Nevertheless, multicultural social policy was funded. In turn, part of the strength of 'ethnic politics' was the fact that the government was paying for it, even to the extent of supporting semi-official ideologues, such as Zubrzycki.

Ethnic politics, then, began as a politics of liberal social reform. As such it was not without its intrinsic merits. In the area of education, for example, specialist English-as-a-Second-Language teaching was a genuine attempt to right the specific disadvantage suffered by children of non-English speaking background. Children of non-English speaking background do suffer specific disadvantage in schools. Multicultural policy in education prescribed social reform, based on an understanding that some groups are disadvantaged. Cultural patterns, viewed by 'ethnic politics' as group life-chances and wider structural relations, needed to be changed.

The social policy of cultural pluralism which came to be the official embodiment of the multicultural response to ethnic politics, in some senses did almost the opposite of ethnic politics. It did not set out to reform society. It merely wished to describe society as it was in order to celebrate its diversity.

A key to understanding cultural pluralism is to begin by trying to work out just what 'culture' in Australia we can be pleasantly 'multi' about. The culture in multiculturalism must be those things which 'already exist' in 'diversity': the 'interesting' and the 'colourful', personal 'lifestyles' and 'relationships', 'identifications' and 'points of view'. These belong to 'the essentially private domain of family and religious belief'.[5] This world is also the realm of 'folk art . . . , dancing, music, craft and literature . . .'[6]

Cultural anthropologists certainly do not understand culture so narrowly. Arguably, this is a pragmatically narrow understanding. Culture happens to be no more and no less than that which we can be happily 'multi' about in Australia. Italian peasant-village life and Polish communism are not culture because we could not really have either in Australia. They are not 'culture' because no-one would suggest that we take multiculturalism that far. But spaghetti and polka are, without doubt, 'culture'. At this point, multiculturalism becomes neither a serious area of social reform policy nor an intellectually worthwhile focus of study.

We have argued that 'ethnic politics' and cultural pluralism are at odds. The two views, however, often exist simultaneously in self-contradiction. On the one hand, the focus is on getting into the same cultural act as the dominant groups; on the other hand, the focus is on maintaining the diversity (which often, and perhaps conveniently, happens not to be a diversity of social equals). On the one hand, there are *de facto* arguments for structural assimilation without tears (with the cultural imperatives and ethos that accompany this); on the other hand, there is an ideology of pluralism, implacably hostile to any suggestion that assimilation might be going on. On the one hand, there is a view that migrants are 'disadvantaged' and need to learn new cultural skills which open up mobility opportunities; on the other hand, the same thing is called 'diversity' which is to be cherished and left alone. On the one hand, social prescription is a rationale for reform; on the other hand, social description is a celebration of what is.

But, having said this, there are also elements of consistency to be found between ethnic politics and cultural pluralism. First, cultural pluralism is a handy and inexpensive solution to the problem of ethnic politics. Second, both cultural pluralism and ethnic politics transpose, albeit by slightly different logics, debates about the plight of minorities from a realm which might in part involve critical structural analysis, to an analysis simply of 'culture' or 'ethnicity'.

The most fundamental question, then, is why bother trivializing the notion of culture? Whatever the inadequacies of a theory such as the reformist vision of ethnic politics, which tries to give all social groups tickets in the lottery of social mobility, at least it admits social disadvantage and wants to find ways of righting it. But when the cultural pluralists attempt to discuss what they mean by the culture we can find in diversity, they shift from social prescription to social description, from the imperatives of reform to a celebration of what exists. At best, multiculturalism is an escape, a consolation for

> the increasing alienation of the individual from the complexities and pressures of modern society. The nation is simply too large, too amorphous, too remote and impersonal to offer a satisfactory basis for wider relationships.[7]

Cultural pluralism, in other words, can help overcome or prevent the insecurity, homogenization and loss of personal identity characteristic of mass society. It is possible to retreat into culture narrowly defined. But there is a sense in which this is precisely the effect of that brand of ethnic politics which merely sees multiculturalism as the removal of 'cultural' or attitudinal barriers from minority groups to play the core cultural game, which itself remains fundamentally unquestioned.

Levels of culture

Of course, culture is more than what can neatly fit within the narrow, pragmatic conception of simple pluralist multiculturalism.[8] It also includes everyday life practices which might conventionally be called political, economic or structural. And even those practices that the simple pluralists find so attractive do not exist independently of wider social pressures. We propose an alternative view of culture which analyses the dynamic relationship of different levels of cultural activity. These are, first, those activities which express the essence of culture and human-ness; second, those variable in history but singular and universal in Australia today (manifest as western industrial society); and third, those life-practices which can exist in variety in the spaces made by western industrial society in Australia today.

First, when we ask what culture is for, we find certain things which unite all people as humans. So, the cultural anthropological definition of culture was initially developed, in part, in a theoretical quest to distinguish humans from animals. Humans characteristically learn their particular forms of social interaction. This means that humans, uniquely, have the ability and freedom to create and change their cultures or social worlds, and not just be bearers of social roles, for whom a blue-print (as with ants) is laid out in their genes.

There are no primordial cultural differences and no ultimately non-communicable cultural gaps. The extraordinary translatability of languages, even if word does not always precisely correspond with word, is but one piece of evidence to support this proposition. Although particular cultures and particular societies are not biologically pre-determined, there is a certain common human inevitability to culture and society. From birth, humans are unable to survive independently. It is this universal fact of sociality that creates the basis of society and the impetus for cultural formation and transmission. All humans have to live in systems of social sharing to satisfy fundamentally common basic needs.

This is not to say that all cultures satisfy needs as well as they could, but to claim that these needs are the reasons why society and culture exist. And these form the basis of universal human standards by which cultures can be judged. Material deprivation, the anti-social maltreatment of one person by another, or insufficient food to eat, for example, are not to be judged by each person's particular cultural standards, but by universal human standards in the essence of what culture is for.

But at a second level, there are important differences in patterns of social organization, and these differences are to be found in the ordinary, taken-for-granted institutions through which basic human needs are satisfied: ways of everyday life, work and welfare, social structures, economic and political institutions, and so on. At this level, there is no real plurality of cultures in Australia today. But what sort of differences could possibly be found at this level if one were to retain the meaning of culture as a whole way of life? Although there is no diversity of culture at this level in Australia today, there have been two major cultures in Australian history, and two cultures within the lives of many families who have migrated to Australia.

The two major cultural forms that have existed on Australian soil are traditional Aboriginal culture and the one that has became dominant during the two centuries since 1788. Traditional Aboriginal hunter-gathering life could hardly be more different from the western industrialism that has developed since the first European settlement. The difference is certainly at a much more profound level than that which just recognizes the difference between say, today's Italian-Australians and Greek-Australians, or the difference between witchety grubs and sausages. And it is a bit late to profess pluralism and multiculturalism now when the fundamental everyday hunter-gathering culture has been all but destroyed by a history of systematic non-pluralism.

Even today, serious offers of genuine pluralism are rarely made. At best, there is a tokenistic respect for such Aboriginal culture as can now exist in plurality without hindering the basic economic intentions of the post-1788 culture. When it comes to the Aborigines, it is very handy to restrict our understanding of culture and dominant social values in Australian history to happy theories of just what happens to be comfortably multicultural in Australia today. It is nice to see Aboriginal art in galleries, but let us not deceive ourselves that this means we are preserving Aboriginal culture, in which, before European domination, production of such a thing as 'art' for 'sale' was inconceivable. Certain cultural phenomena can be misconstrued to be unproblematic expressions of cultural diversity and cultural maintenance. Simple pluralist multiculturalism, as many Aboriginal community leaders themselves recognize, can misread the injustice done to the Aborigines, and misinterpret the amount of plurality really allowed in Australia today. Attempting to 'maintain' Aboriginal languages by recording them, and setting curricula which teach them through institutionalized schooling, to students destined for paid employment, or welfare benefits, is hardly simply a contribution to preserving traditional Aboriginal culture. It certainly creates jobs for linguists and educators; that is, in the extension of the activities of mainstream culture. This is not to say preservation of Aboriginal languages is not worthy or necessary but, again, it is to put in a plea that we do not fool ourselves about what is actually happening historically.

There have also been two cultures at this level in the lives of many migrants to Australia. For example, many people have experienced quite traumatic breaks from peasant-agrarian life to Australia's western industrial society. And often, in some more or less conscious way, they willed the break when they migrated.

At this second level, people newly born in Australia and migrants when they arrive, have to adjust themselves to learning the everyday tactics required for existence in Australian industrial society. If we think of a family migrating to Australia from a village-agricultural culture, there is no practical possibility of them continuing the same life. Besides, historically, people have not migrated to maintain the conditions of village-agricultural society in Australia. They have migrated to leave situations which they might have found socially-culturally unsatisfactory or limiting, for a new culture. This is not to imply that they have simply made a cultural choice in migration. Migration is often just a necessary strategy for reasonable survival. But, to the extent that altered or improved conditions of life are expected, willed, or worked for, there is a process of conscious cultural re-creation in and for a new context.

A hypothetical person from village-agricultural society might find themselves at first in a factory. This is a vastly different way of spending the larger part of one's active life. In an industrial society, the cash economy takes on a greater role and importance. A person needs money to rent or buy any housing at all. If one is not working for payment, one has to have some other monetary support such as welfare payments.

Work itself does not directly provide the things you need, as it had in the village. You have to go to shops or supermarkets to spend the wage earned in your specialized job. And then, how does one relate to one's boss and trade union? How does one use the welfare and health systems? New concepts uproot old ways of mentally organizing the world. New ideas of time have to be learnt: to work by hours and minutes instead of the sun and seasons, to divide the week (work) from the week-end (family), instead of having work and family life constantly inter-related. Dowry and traditional inheritance systems break down. Where in our so-called multicultural society do we find the human geography of a Greek, Lebanese or Laotian village? What happens to the extended family in the face of the demands of occupational mobility? Do migrants from village-agricultural cultures resist consumerism and its structural implications? How easy is it to avoid buying a washing machine when it is now necessary for a wife to work in a job too? What are the implications for a daughter's independence when she gets a job? What happens if you do not master the particular abstract thought needed for basic survival and social interaction (prices, banks, traffic lights, etc)?

In some fundamental senses then, migration to Australia is inevitably going to involve a cultural leap or break if migrants come from a significantly different culture at this level. And, at this level, Australia is not a multicultural society.

Languages, customs and artefacts stretch and change to accommodate the social process of migration when the break for a particular person or class of people is substantial. For example, even if an ex-villager continues to use their mother tongue in the factory and at home in Australia, the language has to deal with issues and activities of the mainstream Australian culture at this second level, and traditional values and practices must be reinterpreted in new circumstances. This can have an effect on the content, meaning and vocabulary of the mother tongue. Likewise, the celebrations of sacred name days in traditional Christian societies can have their religious foundations reduced in a new setting that values them less. Instead they might become part of a new structure of symbols and practices in which the party expresses success and consumerism. Culture and language are never simply maintained. A change in structural context requires new cultural and linguistic solutions to be developed.

At a third level, Australia is indeed a diverse society. As a result of migration, there is a multitude of types of cultural practices in Australia: different types of food, clothing, celebration, music, dance, language, and so on. There is no denying that this enriches life in Australia. Simple pluralist multiculturalism's subject matter — culture at this level — is very worthy of emphasis. For example, whereas language is a communicative tool at the first level and English is the language of elementary social institutions and power in Australia at the second level, at this third level language is something whose sounds we can enjoy and which touches sentiments through shared meanings — yesterday's songs or a mother's turn of phrase. Language conveys special meanings and has special significance. At this level, but at this level alone, English is just a 'community' language, itself used in a series of equally valid genres and registers, and no different or more useful than any other in this respect.

The problem with simple pluralism is that it considers culture and language only at level three. We wish to deny none of the pluralist propositions that people should be enabled to maintain languages because they like them, or because cultural variety of this order is an important value and a human right. Nor would we deny the more academic arguments about the psychological aspects of language in family interaction and identity, or the symbolic significance of language as an instrument of solidarity for minority groups. We simply wish to point out that the picture is larger and more complex than one of linguistic diversity. The arguments about rights and needs cannot be abstracted from the processes in which languages function and interact in the Australian context.

The process of making meaning and community in the migrant context is very complex. It does involve an incorporation of symbols and practices from the new settler's familiar psycho-social landscape. The medium is the message indeed. The gains of multiculturalism in Australia in the form of multilingual media, support for mother-tongue maintenance and so on, cannot now be withdrawn without damage being done to senses of social participation. What happens at level three is very important.

However, the subject matter of level three which so interests pluralist multiculturalism becomes a much more subtle, complex and problematic phenomenon when it is seen to be related to structural issues of migration at level two. Modern industrial societies are large and complex in historically specific ways, such that effective understanding and manipulation necessitates a particular sort of abstraction; map-reading, detailed laws and regulations, intercommunication through telephone or mass media systems. Large, structural relations need to be perceived if one is not to be completely marginalized. For all of this, a new language is required, not so much in terms of meanings but in functional content. For example, providing translation services for taxation, and the law, or even mounting multi-lingual courses explaining Australian society, pre-supposes that all immigrants, irrespective of their particular life-history, had the appropriate semantic framework for manipulation of these new life forms in their place of origin. For the middle-class, educated, 'modern' city-dwellers, that might be the case. But for the very substantial proportion of Australia's non-English speaking immigrant population, this is not so. Indeed, it frequently becomes the case that some new immigrants move between domestic interchange in their first language and the use of English to explain new institutions, technologies and social relations, rather than take on the forms of their language of origin which express and manipulate life in advanced industrial quarters in their place of origin.

Minority languages might be maintained, but the very space they inhabit, the functions they perform and their consequent social character are defined by the dominant culture at level two. They predominantly become languages of domestic, private or spare-time usage. They need not be that way and are not like that in their place of origin. But with the particular place they have in Australian society, they frequently (especially for second generations) become that way. Also, because languages other than English become unnecessary to elementary survival, they are sited in such a way that strategies for their maintenance have to become self-conscious rather than inevitable and unexceptional. One might wish for a society in which a plurality of languages were to be used equally in every sphere of life. But no one has seriously proposed this.

Moreover, the pluralist celebrates diversity at level three as if the diversity were a truly independent realm and a diversity of equals. Our duty, it follows, is simply to maintain languages as they are for the sake of their preservation.

In an holistic view of the situation, there is nothing necessarily problematic about the goal of multiculturalism or multi-lingualism so long as it does not simultaneously involve reproducing structures of inequality in which some cultures and linguistic-cognitive forms are in practice adequate to social participation, and others not. This does not deny that there are different spheres of social participation, for which there are different languages or forms of language. Our primary task is to assess their general social function. This applies equally to English. And we must be careful not to limit our view of social function in such as way that tokens or gestures seem adequate, in the hope, perhaps, that regardless of the linguistic outcome, some psychological sense of self-esteem or tolerance of others will come simply through institutional approval of a language.

Some forms of cultural pluralism, in sum, are less than adequate readings of culture and society. They involve trivializing cultural differences as stereotypes (spaghetti and polka); and removing the issues of immigration, Aboriginality and cultural difference generally from the social-structural realm to the cultural realm defined in colourful, celebratory and apolitical terms. They also frequently involve assumptions about a primordial folk, often based on imported, exclusionary, nationalist ideologies; an acritical assumption that cultural preservation and the maintenance of traditions are inherently a good thing; a reproduction of cultural traditions which in their own time-honoured processes of self-definition are racist and sexist; and the affirmation of traditional cultural boundaries and senses of superiority (Maintain our culture; Don't marry out). Most crucial for our argument in this book, however, through policies of cultural pluralism the state is now actively supporting forms of cultural identity whose defining boundaries are not those of the nation-state itself. This is a striking departure from the whole spirit and practice of assimilation. The move to cultural pluralism is but one symptom of the declining viability of nationalist ideologies.

Blainey and the New Right

Against the cultural pluralist analysis of multiculturalism, we have seen emerging in the 1980s a New Right which is very perceptive of many of the weaknesses of pluralist multiculturalism and which aims, in essence, to revive the nationalist message of assimilation to overcome Australia's social and economic woes.

However, their 'solution', an unimaginative and regressive return to the old assimilating nationalism, is probably no longer viable. The causes of the end of nationalism are so profound that more imagination than ever is required to construct an ideology of community that fits neatly within the boundaries of the nation-state. Historian Geoffrey Blainey, who many commentators align with the New Right but who in many ways is significantly different from them, puts an 'historical' perspective to this view:

> Sir Henry Parkes, a father of the Commonwealth of Australia said in 1890s: 'The crimson thread of kinship runs through us all.'
> That crimson thread is vital for any nation, but in the last six years

there has been a growing concern at the way in which Australian governments, perhaps with lofty aims, have cut the crimson threads. The cult of the immigrants, the emphasis on separateness for ethnic groups, the wooing of Asia and the shunning of Britain are part of this thread-cutting. The disowning of our own past is also a part. Attempts to depict Australian history as mainly a story of exploitation, of racial violence, of oppressions and conflict have a measure of truth, but contain a larger measure of untruth. Again and again Australia is depicted as a bonanza — ready made — that was snatched from the Aboriginals. But the Australia of the Aboriginals, distinctive as were its achievements, was not a bonanza. Generations of Australians since 1788 have developed this land and its resources, applying sweat and grit and ingenuity. Asian immigrants had the opportunity to come several hundred years ago, but they had no incentive to come. Australia was not worth colonizing.

The multicultural message ignores this truth. It tends to see Australia as simply a vast piece of good fortune that should increasingly be shared with the world. But Australia will not remain a piece of good fortune, its standards of living will not be sufficient to attract many immigrants, and its political and social stability will not attract the essential capital if immigration policies slowly destroy our sense of cohesion and our pride in our past.[9]

Australian national identity is at a crisis point. Blainey reflects upon this in a way which raises fundamental questions about Australian history and national identity. Against the soul-searching and equivocation that comes with multiculturalism and the critical reappraisal of the effects of the establishment of an industrial society upon land previously possessed by gatherers and hunters, Blainey advocates a return to an older, simpler story of Australia, a story more likely to rally the nation around a cohesive national pride. In this story, the established European settlers of Australia have a peculiar claim to the place, for their efforts in the development of its resources and their achievement of industrialism.

Blainey is a crucial reference point for any reading of racism and Australian identity in the late 1980s. He is crucial in an immediate, political sense for being the 'authority' on Australian history and on popular cultural identity which was at the heart of the immigration debate of 1984. He is crucial because his work involves not simply the crude fulminations we hear from the likes of Bruce Ruxton, President of the Victorian branch of the Returned Servicemen's League, but an elaborated historical vision. Blainey also combines, in a very revealing way, issues of multiculturalism as the product of mass immigration with the question of Australian Aboriginal land rights. To introduce this discussion, we will begin by examining the pivotal immigration debate of 1984.

It is not usual for throw-away remarks made in speeches to Rotarians of Warrnambool to create much of a stir, but Blainey's closing remarks to such a speech on 18 March 1984 hit the national headlines and kept Blainey's name there for most of that year. He was touching a raw public nerve.

Blainey presented himself as worried about what he considered to be excessive 'Asian' immigration. As his position emerged in the media debate, it became obvious he was concerned that cultural differences could divide Australia. According to Blainey, the old White Australia Policy used offensive language, but its substance had made a lot of sense. We now rightly denounce that policy, he argued, but we also often exaggerate its faults in a fit of excessive guilt. White Australia was based on what Blainey considered to be the perfectly reasonable assumption that immigrants should assimilate. The new 'Asian Australia Policy', on the other hand, was equally offensive in its insensitivity towards Australian public opinion.[10]

In the neighbourhood, a 'myriad of little things' contribute to growing resentment: the smell of goat's meat, noodles drying on the clothes line and phlegm on the footpath. And the self-same 'ethnics' who reduce the desirability of the neighbourhood end up driving flash cars while ordinary Australians continue to suffer rising unemployment and declining standards of living.[11] Blainey does not say this is his own opinion. He simply speaks from his 'knowledge' of Australian history and for popular sentiments. 'It's easy for me in my secure job to say I welcome Asian immigrants; I do welcome them, but they do not compete with me for work and they do not alter the way of life where I live.'[12] He is the historical realist arguing against the trendy and affluent multicultural idealists.

Historian and populist come together. If any lesson is to be learnt from Australian history, says Blainey, it is that immigration should be reduced in times when the economic climate is depressed. He claims to speak for the 'working class', 'traditional Australians', 'the poorer people', 'the least educated section of society', 'the average Australian', 'everyday Australians'.[13] In the 1950s these people might have been suspicious of new immigrants, but their fears were allayed by the obvious merits of immigration. After the Second World War and the fall of Singapore, Australians learnt the simple lesson that the nation needed population if it was to survive. Then, the newcomers' culture was not so different, there was full employment and the ghettos were neither as tight nor as large.[14] A lesson to be learnt from the nineteenth century was that concentrations of Asians, even when their numbers proportional to the whole population were small, could produce serious conflicts.

If it is not enough that this populism represents a superficial and journalistic mode for reading history, Blainey actually appears to get his facts wrong at crucial points. On his overall interpretation of Australia's post-war immigration programme: the 1950s were not, despite his claims, a period of popular acceptance of immigration; nor was 1984, in comparison, a period of particular disapproval of immigration. And, on his more general point that this was the first time in Australian history when unemployment and significant immigration have coincided, the 1920s is just one contrary example. Also, countering another of Blainey's points, many of the apparently acceptable immigrants of the 1950s were more different from his Australian norm (Southern European peasants, for example) than many of the recent Indochinese immigrants (those of the professional, urban middle-class background, for example).

In the numerous public opinion polls of 1984, concern was expressed about the relation of immigration to unemployment, but 'Asian'-ness itself was not, as Blainey supposed, seen to be the problem.[15] In a long-term historical sense, too, the opinion polls seem to contradict Blainey. Even though the nature of the questions asked varies, a comprehensive listing of opinion poll results on the issue of immigration since 1943, put together by the Department of Immigration and Ethnic Affairs, shows, if anything, precisely an opposite move by the recession period of the 1980s to that predicted by Blainey. It seems that, slowly and progressively, the range of acceptable immigrants broadens in the post-war period.[16] Even at the height of the 1984 debate, Blainey's empirical 'public opinion' failed to materialize. Unions opposed him. Unemployed workers opposed him. The conservative opposition parties were hesitant even to associate themselves with the moderately phrased Blainey line. Only such dubious representatives of the 'people' as Ruxton, some sections of the Liberal and National parties (equivocally), Hugh Morgan of Western Mining Company, National Action and Brigadier P.J. Greville, publicly supported him.

Had Blainey spoken in the mid-1960s his views would have gone unnoticed as unexceptional. Blainey's newsworthiness was for advocating a return, as a respectable public person, to the old assimilationist Australia, against the dramatic rewriting of conventional wisdoms about cultural differences in the 1970s and 1980s. The furore around Blainey and the fact that he found no respectable or official support, is indicative of how much Australia had changed by the mid-1980s.

Blainey placed himself unequivocally on the side of the old culturally and historically self-confident Australia of industrial progress and national development. Aborigines and immigrants, in the last analysis, had to become part of that Australia. And, at the level of identity, the bearers of that industrial society very understandably require a unitary identity. 'As human beings we will all continue to have our preferences and loyalties and affinities.'

Although Blainey achieved the highest media profile, he is not the only person to have attacked multiculturalism. It has also been under considerable attack from an emerging New Right. The main organs of this loose grouping have been the magazine *Quadrant*, *The Australian* and *The Bulletin*. Although without formal organization, the New Right has a number of intellectual focal points, most notably the Institute for Public Affairs and the Centre for Independent Studies. Blainey has frequently been classified as a member of the New Right, but he has disavowed the term, stressing the moderation, even-handedness, and just plain historical commonsense of his views. And, in many ways, this disassociation contains significant elements of truth. The New Right assault on multiculturalism has been more sustained, although less publicized; it has been less populist and much more 'intellectual'; and it fits into a broader and more coherent critique of Australian society.

Most importantly, however, the New Right, unlike Blainey, by and large supports significant immigration as part of the project of continuing development. For example, Frank Knopfelmacher, a long-time New Right critic of multiculturalism has said he 'strongly favours Vietnamese immigration to Australia because, as former military allies, we are honour-bound to help them in adversity and because they are splendid migrants in every respect'.[17] Prominent supporters of this position, whether or not their larger world view corresponds to that of the New Right, include such diverse and public figures as former Queensland Premier Johannes Bjelke-Petersen, media magnate Kerry Packer and former Western Australian Premier Brian Burke. In our reading of the New Right, however, we will concentrate on its intellectuals.

Ironically, the virtue of Indochinese immigrants is precisely their ready assimilability into 'Anglomorph' culture. From the standpoint of political and moral values, Knopfelmacher writes, Anglomorph societies are superior to all existing others. This is also why immigrants come here and particularly why, given their experience of communism, Indochinese appear to be so happy to join a society based essentially on an English heritage: freedom and order, individualism, technical progress, greater morality than elsewhere in public life, and so on.[18]

The New Right recognizes and abhors the crisis of unitary national identity. It puts this down in large measure to the destructive influence of a 'new class' of trendy left intellectuals and public servants. By the late 1980s, wrote David Barnett in *The Bulletin*, there were thousands of government employees in the multicultural industry with a 'vested interest in perpetuating separate ethnic identities'. The best slogan the Bicentennial could come up with was the banal 'Living Together'. The perceptions of this New Right are frequently very shrewd, even if Anglomorphy is a rather bizarre aspiration for Indochinese immigrants, in contra-distinction to the somewhat different aspiration to success in the competitive world of wage labour and commodity production. 'Hard multiculturalism', in order to preserve 'ethnic integrity', it is pointed out, is equally liable to assist in the reproduction of traditions and values that 'are at least as grotesquely ignorant and as racist as sexist and as bigoted as any that can be squeezed from the most appalling of 'ocker'.'[19] Furthermore, as L.J.M. Cooray argues in *Quadrant*, multiculturalism is based on a 'retrogressive conception of culture', static and seeking to retard, naively and against inevitable pressures, the process of cultural interaction and evolution. He goes on to characterize the holders of multicultural theories as 'patronizing Anglomorphs' and points, by way of example, to the 'difference between teaching language for its educational value and teaching it in pursuance of the illusory goals of multiculturalism.'[20] This critique of multiculturalism, identifying its inherent conservatism, is more incisive than Blainey's, forcing its limitations to absurdity and locating the problem in the more general context of the rise of liberal pluralism as the dominant ideological paradigm.

Ways of interpreting cultural difference in general are eminently transferable, as they are based, at root, more in one's conception of oneself than in the real nature of the 'other'. Assimilation, then, both for Aborigines and for immigrants, and regardless of the depth of the contrast between these two groups, represented a view of the historical superiority and mission of industrial society. Insofar as this was strongly founded on an association of 'races' and 'civilizations', it has to be termed 'racist'.

Both Blainey and the New Right represent revived versions of this conception of Australian identity. At the most fundamental level, both Blainey and the New Right recommend an ideology of unitary identity and self-assurance about the superiority of the industrial society in which we live. Partly reminiscent of the glories of English colonial ideology, both inject an element of English-ness into their characterization of this society. Both advocate assimilation as the most desirable approach to cultural difference. In articulating these views, they advocate a return to the past in critical appraisal of the development of multiculturalism and cultural pluralism generally. These are the roots of their brand of racism.

At more superficial levels, Blainey falls into modes of discourse which are more immediately and inevitably racist. Diagnosing the visible phenotypical and cultural differences of 'Asian'-ness as the significant problem of racism, both in nineteenth-century Australia and today, is to accept at face value the racist interpretative framework of some of the historical and social actors. Visible differences are not themselves the problem. The problem is the ideology of racism as a means of (mis)-interpreting social division. Blainey follows those social actors he considers to be significant into the misconception of a supposed reality of 'race' as the problem rather than 'racism' as ideology.

The New Right, on the other hand, while equally convinced of the virtues and supposedly inevitable realities of assimilation, evidently think the cultural difference of 'Asian'-ness less great than Blainey and thus that 'Anglomorphy', for any immigrant convinced of the virtues of the free enterprise society, is a viable and desirable process. Of course, here are very obvious assumptions about the incompatibility and undesirability of continuing cultural difference, in which frequently racist assumptions are not so deeply submerged.

Blainey and the New Right are not simply temporary and unpalatable social commentators. They reiterate the official policy and the dominant popular ideology of the decades up to the mid-1970s and reflect some fundamental structural and cultural processes which still persist, despite some of the pretensions of the happy ideology of cultural pluralism of the 1980s.

The actual historical processes and policies of assimilation which they reflect and advocate were racist in some important ways. Assimilation took two somewhat contradictory directions. On the one hand, there was an assurance about continuing difference so as not to threaten working conditions and living standards. Immigrants, for example, would not take desirable jobs from established Australian workers. This assurance of difference went right through to directives that immigrants were not to be allowed, deceptively, to take on Anglo-sounding names.[21] On the other hand, assimilation was an ideology of sameness which could only reproduce or recreate popular memories and traditions of racism. Migrants, ostensibly, would become normal Australians, and as quickly as possible appear as just the same as the rest. This was merely a cultural argument, a reassurance against racist fears of difference, that singular Australian-ness would prevail at the level of observable cultural phenomena. Precisely the assurance of structural differentiation limited the project of assimilation to the cultural arena narrowly defined, thus guaranteeing a racism of structural differentiation.

Moreover, assimilation was racist, even within its narrowly cultural perspective, because it was based on ever-present assumptions about the greater virtue of dominant cultural practices to the extent that different others should simply be incorporated so that much of their previous difference becomes invisible.

As much as the policy recreated racism, there were also elements of assimilation, however, which, either in their long-term structural impact or in their ideology, were non-racist. Simply the extent of migration, and the successful incorporation of immigrants into an albeit socially segmented Australian economic boom, accidentally provided cultural lessons to a previously relatively homogeneous Australian population. Assimilation may well have used racist ideology and social prognosis to sell immigration to the Australian working class, but the long-term impact of the migration programme has been to reduce racism at the cultural level and to contribute to a crisis of singular Australian identity. The empirical proof of the pudding is the failure of Blainey to gain substantial public support or to affect immigration policy. Furthermore, even within assimilation as a culturalist ideology, there is, contradictorily, a non-racist strand: 'They are different; they can be like us; we can live together; differences do not constitute an immutable threat.'

The critical contrast of this cultural racism to the biological-reductionist racism of English colonial ideology is incapsulated in British sociologist Martin Barker's distinction of the 'old' from the 'new' racism. What Barker calls the 'new racism' of the 1970s and 1980s mixes phenotypical and cultural obviousness as supposed causes of social division. Mrs Thatcher, in a radio broadcast leading up to her winning her first election as British Prime Minister, pointed to the 'understandable' feeling of insecurity many people had, given all the visible differences in the street: the turbans, presumably, as well as the skin colours. Blainey is an excellent example of this 'culturally aware' new racism. The 'problem' of 'Asians' is simply their unassimilated obvious-ness, be it phenotypical or cultural. The distinction that many wish to make between racism and enthnocentrism is in this case not only empirically very difficult to make, but also implicitly admits that the one is really about a reality that can be called 'race' and the other about another reality called 'culture'. In fact the 'race' and 'culture' of each is equally a fiction, an immediate appearance being made into a root social cause. Racism, to reiterate our earlier arguments, should be defined not by its actors' reference but by its function as ideology.

Conclusion

In Chapters Six and Seven, we have put forward an extended argument about four major moments in the unfolding, conflict-ridden history of Australian identity. Only two of these could be called nationalist in the sense defined in Chapter Six: the ideology of assimilation of the post-Second World War decades and its recent revival by the so-called New Right. The question remains, where are we now? Who will win the present contest between multicultural orthodoxy and the New Right nationalist revival?

As we argued in Chapter Six on the question of the demise of nationalism, structural changes in the world economy and the internationalization of the culture industry reduce the importance of identification with the nation-state. In the late 1980s, with the contracting welfare state, the increasing privatization of enterprises and development projects previously undertaken by the state, and the internationalization of basic economic structures, it is no longer so necessary to construct an imagined community that fits neatly within the boundaries of the nation-state. These structural phenomena, despite the severity of the economic and cultural crises that the New Right have cleverly put their fingers upon, are hardly ones that nationalism can erase. In other words, despite the intensity of the social crisis, there are profound reasons why the New Right's wishful imaginings, their nostalgic desire for a return to the good old days, are a long way off the mark. With cultural pluralism riddled with its own weaknesses, not the least of which is the loss of cohesive communal purpose beyond the individual and the particular, and with the New Right espousing a return which becomes less and less realistic as late industrial society relentlessly pursues its course, the result of this contest for our hearts and minds is very much an open question.

Pluralism, despite the New Right, is still the order of the day, which is why the Bicentennial is such an implausible exercise.

The 1987 Anzac day issue of the *Sydney Morning Herald* serves to reinforce this observation. As Benedict Anderson argues that death in war is the ultimate symbol of the ideological power of nationalism, so representation of Anzac day in the Australian context would seem to be a good indicator of the relative strength and nature of nationalism. The cover story, 'No Grave can be Big Enough for Men like These', recites the traditional nationalist litany, quoting cliches about the men of Gallipoli from Manning Clark, C.E.W. Bean and Patsy Adam-Smith. Yet the same article gives equal space to the comments of Turkish historians and local villagers. Further on in the paper, the traditional nationalist story is destroyed by recounting the experience of Vietnam. Quoting a veteran,

> I went to Vietnam willingly. Make no mistake about that. But I took with me the youthful visions of war, of clear-cut frontlines, of heroic deeds, of mateship, and of battles with victors and the vanquished. Comic-book images of Tobruk, the Somme, Gallipoli and the Kokoda Trail. The spirit of Anzac forged on a thousand battlefields. Honourable war. Noble and splendid . . .
> I was 19 years old. I knew nothing . . .
> My son, aged eight, asked me if he would have to fight for his country. I told him, no. Australia and Australians weren't worth it. I would break his knee-cap first.[22]

Relativizing the experience of war, another article tells of the conditions suffered by Italian, German and Japanese prisoners of war in Australia. Interspersed were articles on D. H. Lawrence's *Kangaroo*, describing the transmutation of returned First World War diggers into proto-fascists; and a review of Henry Reynolds's new book, *Frontier*, providing more evidence of the nature of European-Aboriginal relations and arguments for the inalienable right of

Aborigines to land ownership. The old, singular ideology of Australian-ness, even its Anzac legend, is now significantly qualified.

Where does this leave the Bicentenary? Ronald Conway, in the *Sydney Morning Herald* one week after Anzac Day, wrote of 'our Great Bicentennial Mess, presided over by an authority groping for some threads of Australianity, but badgered at every turn by minority voices which declare that 1788-and-all-that represents an Anglo-Celtic colonial aberration. Worthier to be cursed than celebrated.'[23] And Craig McGregor writes that in the Australia of year 199, the New Right ascends in the face of a

> New Politics based upon movements which arose in the 1970s and departed from the usual party alignments; it includes the women's movement, the anti-nuclear and peace movement, Aboriginal rights, the sexual liberation movements, community action, and the conservation movement.[24]

As yet, the New Right has not managed to forge its new nationalism either as a popular or officially acceptable and workable alternative. The Right has a chance of success, however, given the profundity and seriousness of the loss of the larger communal purpose which it correctly senses. It is almost too much of a cliché to point to drug-taking, levels of adolescent existential angst and general adolescent resignation. But a revived assimilating nationalism is not only a repugnant alternative for its arrogant and insensitive obliteration of real differences in history and experience; it is also an almost impossible alternative given the dual process of world structural-cultural unification and the growing significance of sub-cultural identifications and forms of politics. Both of these trends, pulling contradictorily in opposite directions, make ideologies of singular and readily definable nation-ness less and less plausible.

The question remains, however: Where do we go? What forms of communal identity are possible in the Australia of the late twentieth century? We turn to these questions in our concluding chapter.

Notes

1. New South Wales Department of Education, *Our Multicultural Society*, Sydney 1983, p.53.
2. Victorian Ministry of Education, *Aboriginal Studies Resources List: Primary*, July 1986.
3. Alan Ashbolt, 'Godzone: myth and reality', *Meanjin*, Vol.25, No.4, December 1966, p.374.
4. Richard White, *Inventing Australia*, Sydney: George Allen & Unwin 1981, pp.vi-vii, 168-169.
5. Australian Council on Population and Ethnic Affairs, *Multiculturalism for All Australians: Our Developing Nationhood*, Canberra 1982, p.16.
6. Australian Ethnic Affairs Council, *Australia as a Multicultural*

Society, Canberra 1977, p.6.
7.   P.W. Matthews, 'Multuralism and education', *Education News*, 16:10 1979, p.16.
8.   See Mary Kalantzis, Bill Cope and Diana Slade, *The Language Question: The Maintenance of Languages other than English*, Canberra: AGPS 1986.
9.   Geoffrey Blainey, *All for Australia*, Sydney: Methuen Haynes 1984, pp.158-160.
10.   Blainey, p.7.
11.   Blainey, pp.121,131-132.
12.   Blainey, 'The Asianization of Australia', Melbourne *Age*, 20 March 1984.
13.   Blainey, *All for Australia*, p.1, 'The Asianization of Australia'.
14.   Blainey, *All for Australia*, p.130.
15.   'Critics of multiculturalism', paper presented to the Australian Institute for Multicultural Affairs National Research Conference, May 14-16 1986.
16.   *MIMEO*, Department of Immigration and Ethnic Affairs.
17.   Quoted by David Humphries, 'Professor Blainey explains himself', Melbourne *Age*, 20 March 1984.
18.   Frank Knopfelmacher, 'The case against multiculturalism', in: R. Manne (ed.), *The New Conservtism in Australia*, Melbourne: Oxford University Press 1982, pp.40-64.
19.   David Barnett, 'Dividing Australia: how Government money for ethnics is changing our nation', *The Bulletin*, 18 February 1986, pp.58-62; Lauchlan Chipman, 'The menace of multiculturalism', *Quadrant*, October 1980, pp.3-6.
20.   L.J.M. Cooray, 'Multiculturalism in Australia: who needs it?', *Quadrant*, April 1986, pp.27-29.
21.   Ellie Vasta, Ph.D research project, University of New England.
22.   *Sydney Morning Herald*, 25 April 1987, p.41.
23.   Ronald Conway, 'Strangers in our own land', *Sydney Morning Herald*, 2 May 1987.
24.   Craig McGregor, 'Australia: Year 199', *Sydney Morning Herald*, 2 May 1987.

8.
Community Without Nation?

In this book we have looked at the development of a multi-ethnic society in Australia, and have outlined the problems this brings for the definition of the nation. We have examined the various ideologies developed in response — in particular at racism, assimilation and multiculturalism — and have shown their consequences for the policies and institutional structures of the state. We have drawn attention to parallels in the use of migrant labour and the development of ethnic minorities between Australia and other advanced western industrial countries. The most obvious specific features of the Australian case are the relatively large volume of immigration and settlement, and the policy of extending citizenship and full civil rights to all migrants who want them. In this final chapter, we will draw some conclusions from our analysis, and examine the various options open to Australians in the decades ahead.

Homogeneity, difference and the state

The world history of the last few decades has been marked by a contradiction: on the one hand technological change, improving communications and the growing integration of the world market are making the world smaller and more homogeneous; on the other hand, there has been a revived emphasis on difference, whether in terms of individual life-styles, group cultural identities, or assertion of national uniqueness. The 'ethnic explosion' observed around the world embodies this contradiction: ethnicity, which purports to derive from the common history and traditions of a specific group, arises in the context of states which are increasingly all-embracing, both in size and in function. The Australian model of multiculturalism, with its complex and ambiguous balance between separatism of the varied groups, and cohesion of society as a whole, is one — relatively successful and peaceful — way of managing this contradiction. Yet it is inherently unstable, because the institution on which it is premised — the nation-state as the fundamental human collective

— has itself become questionable. This is apparent on three inter-related levels: the economic, the cultural and the political.

The economic level is the most obvious: the central form of organization of the contemporary economy is becoming less and less the nation-state and more and more the international institutions of industry and finance. In early free enterprise industrial development (such as nineteenth-century Britain) the state was meant to abstain from economic intervention, merely using its power to regulate social conflict and to maintain appropriate military forces and foreign policies. In the imperialist phase of industrial development (such as in Germany up to 1918) the state took an active role in a partnership with industrial and financial capital to set up large-scale production units, to capture markets, and to contain the labour movement. In the welfare (or Keynesian) phase of world develop-ment (in most advanced economies in the period 1945 to about 1970) the state was active in regulating the economy, providing the infras-tructure needed for production and containing social conflict through policies of full employment and social security. Woe betide any state today that tries to take such an interventionist role. It will meet with an investment strike by transnational industry and finance, a capital flight by national industry and, should it try to take protectionist measures, disciplinary action by world economic insti-tutions like the International Monetary Fund. The leeway for national economic policies has become very narrow indeed, as the Labor Government has found since 1983.

There are two possible courses for a reformist government: to toe the line laid down by international forces, reducing social justice policies to marginal redistributions between the employed and the poor; or to seek a completely new economic strategy, based on popular control and participation. The Hawke Government has chosen the former path. This reduces national economic policy to a mere interpretation of the parameters laid down by a seemingly objective and all-powerful world market. The government has become an administrative organ entrusted with the task of providing the legal, fiscal, transport, administrative and social infrastructure needed for the smooth functioning of the Australian part of the world economy.

The homogenization of world culture has taken a similar course: the shift of cultural production from the household or the local community to the world factory profoundly affects our ways of life. Most people wear jeans, drink Coca-Cola, use electronic media and eat factory-made food. Even the most committed 'Greenie' critic of modern culture flies by jet to protest conventions, and returns home to listen to 1960s 'hippie' rock on a compact disc player. The British eat spaghetti, the Africans white bread, the Asians wiener schnitzel; but it all derives from the plants of world agri-business. The point is that homogenization actually makes differentiation both possible and meaningless: we can all get everything everywhere, but it has ceased to have any real cultural significance. Whatever we do is a celebration of the cultural dominance of the great international industrial structure, but we can kid ourselves on the basis of appearances that our culture or sub-culture is different. As difference loses its meaning, our need for it as a focus of identity becomes ever greater, as do our acts of self-deception. The attempt to preserve static, pre-industrial forms of ethnic culture is an obvious example of this.

The increasing integration of the world results in a simultaneous homogenization and fragmenting of culture. We are all in the same boat, but this does not mean that there is a single and universal political answer. Socialist and communist movements of the past could point to a goal relevant to all workers and, in the final analysis, to all human beings (because all were destined to become workers): the abolition of capitalism. In a world where socialist movements have failed in the most advanced countries, and where the 'real socialism' of many less advanced countries does not appear as an attractive option, the politics of radical opposition has tended to become fragmented. The universalist party has been replaced by the single-issue movements, based on gender, ethnicity, sexual preference, environmental concern, the wish for peace and so on. These movements are interlinked, and people move between them, but they are not capable of putting forward a viable global economic and political alternative.

If the nation-state is increasingly irrelevant on both the economic and cultural levels, what is the point of having it at all, and what is its political task? The leading apologists of the modern world economy tell us that its rationality lies in its very anarchy. The neo-classical economists have returned to the idea of an 'invisible hand', which secures optimum efficiency in production and distribution (not optimum equality, of course). Any state intervention in this market mechanism is seen as disasterous. A world state would be a threat to the freedom of the market. So the economically weak nation-state remains a functional political unit. It is able to a limited extent to develop and maintain national ideologies and loyalties. It can manage class and racial conflicts. It can provide systems of social security, education and training needed to develop mass loyalty and to socialize the working population. Briefly: the nation-state is still the most effective agency of social control.

Problems of the Australian nation-state

But as the nation-state loses many of its former functions and powers, becoming more and more an empty shell, it suffers a crisis of legitimacy. It needs powerful ideologies to shore up its crumbling walls. Where are they to be found? Return to traditional ideas of national greatness is one possibility: reassertion of heroic episodes of history (the founding of the nation) and the restating of central values (the family, free enterprise, democracy). A war is a traditional way out. Who thought it would still work until Mrs Thatcher sent the Fleet to the Malvinas, and Reagan invaded Grenada, bombed Libya and mined the harbours of Nicaragua? Military might still appears a central component of the idea of national greatness in the USA. Reagan's main strength was his capacity to wield such images. Racism has proved a viable, though limited, ideology for post-Keynesian society in Britain, France, West Germany and other European nations. Economic strength and efficiency remain powerful stereotypes in West Germany and Japan.

In thinking about Australian nationalism as a particular phenomenon, it is as well to think first about nationalism as a general phenomenon.

According to the literature reviewed in Chapter Six, nationalism is heavily reliant on symbolic manifestations which create a sense of community (overarching or even negating class or gender divisions) and immortality (in which the loss of self in death is palliated by the continuing existence of the nation). Its essential references are to primordiality, nature and exclusion. The nation is constructed not only around the presumed existence of a 'race', culture or language but also around the *origin* of that entity in semi-mythological (non-historical) time, and around some unique and generally superior national destiny. Almost invariably the nation is constructed in a process of conflict with other nations over the question of territory. We speak of geographical areas as 'achieving nationhood' or 'joining the family of nations'.

In terms of these characteristics it can be seen that some nations may develop a sense of community and cohesion which is extremely strong in the sense that the national myth is explicit, passionately internalized by the bulk of the population and largely immune from question, dissent or satire at the level of public discourse. Conversely, some states which are recognized as nations develop no such integrative bonds or, at least, very weak ones.

In each individual case only a study of the history of this nation reveals why the sinews binding together the 'imagined community' are of steel or of cotton wool: but some generalizations can be made.

First, nationalism tends to be most intense and least problematic in those states which 'achieved nationhood' as a result of some relatively short and easily identifiable historical trauma. The war of liberation, the war of independence, the great patriotic war are the most potent symbols of nationalism. Anderson is quite correct to stress the iconographic power of the tomb of the unknown soldier, but how much more powerful an icon is the statue of the unknown soldier who 'fell' in the creation (or heroic defence) of the motherland or fatherland than he whose demise occurred in the process of slaughtering Zulus, Ashantis or Kikuyu?

Indeed, in some nations formed out of the breakdown of European imperialism, a revolutionary war of independence has been proposed as the essential crucible of the nation. This was the view, for example, of Amilcar Cabral, the leader and theoretician of Guinean independence, and it is also a dominant strain in the writings of Tito and Mao.

Second, nationalism is strengthened by the ability to legitimize itself by reference to a period of continuity extending back to some prehistoric (or quasi-historical) time. The posturings of the Mussolinis and Shah Pahlevis about the immemorial ancestries of their regimes made no historical sense, of course, but at an emotional level they were both functional and potent. If the nation is immortal it is as well that it should be primordial: if it has no visible end it is strengthened by having no proximate beginning. Also it should be stressed that historically located beginnings are not incompatible with an ideology of primordiality. Ireland did not become a nation after the events of 1916-21: it became 'a nation once again'. Indeed, the sense of periodic destruction of the state apparatus which exemplifies the nation is in itself a powerful image of the primordial strength of the nation. It lives on even though ground down and subjugated and national destiny is fulfilled as it emerges to 'freedom'.

Third, the sense of national identity can be strengthened by investing in a particular state a consciousness of unique responsibility for some chiliastic mission. The sense of being the 'leader of the free world' and the unique repository of democratic values is one obvious case in point, and the carnage that has taken place on the Persian Gulf is another. Perhaps this spirit is best summed up by Salman Rushdie who observed that Pakistani soldiers were advantaged in conflicts with Indians since the former faced the prospect of martyrdom followed by instant entry to paradise while the latter could look forward only to reincarnation (possibly in a form even less desirable than that of an Indian infantryman).

Are these sorts of nationalist option open to Australia? The answer is, in general, no. Moreover, we are fortunate that that is the case. Australia has got through two hundred years without too much of the violent, the dramatic and the heroic. It is a patriot's never-never land: no colonial liberation struggle, no revolution, no civil war, no wars with foreign powers fought on its own soil. The struggles to subjugate the Aborigines have been collectively suppressed from the national memory. Of course, Australia has had some history as part of the British Empire, and it was in that guise that Australians died heroically at Gallipoli. But the most important battle to preserve Australian nationhood was fought vicariously, through the agency of the US Navy in the Coral Sea. The Eureka Stockade and the struggle of nineteenth-century democrats for Federation are not the stuff of which national legends are made. They cannot be mentioned in the same breath as the American War of Independence or the storming of the Bastille. And the idea that an Australian Prime Minister might start a war to pull the nation together is too laughable to mention. Sending a gunboat to Suva was not on, even just before a federal election.

Shared heritage and culture is also not for Australia, a viable ideology of the nation. The reasons, as we have described throughout this book, are the increasingly vocal claims of the Aborigines to cultural integrity and the post-war immigration programme, which has created a situation in which around a quarter of the population are of non-British origin. People of British descent are still a majority, but an ideology which excludes such a sizeable proportion of the population is fundamentally flawed. Moreover, the British tradition is all too ambivalent in Australia: first, because of the convict stigma attached to initial settlement; second, because of the long drawn-out struggle to gain a separate Australian identity — summed up in 'anti-pommie' feeling.

Economic strength and prosperity is no longer a candidate for the role of unifying ideology. It did play that role for many years: in the post-war boom, 'the Australian Way' was defined in terms of consumerism. Good tucker, an owner-occupied house on a quarter-acre block, a car and perhaps a boat were symbols of Australian-ness which were open to all irrespective of ethnic origin. With real wages declining, housing costs rising, and — for the first time — the percentage of owner-occupiers falling, material prosperity can no longer be a key to national unity.

Racism

What about racism as an instrument for securing social solidarity? By drawing the boundaries of the nation in an exclusionary way, racism creates an 'imagined community', drawing people together through affective links which transcend conflicting socio-economic interests. Racism has had this function for most of Australian history. The White Australia Policy was a central element of Australian nationhood from the late nineteenth century right through to the 1960s. If we look overseas, we see that racism has been a traditional and frequent instrument for constructing national solidarity in crisis situations. It currently plays this role in several advanced industrial countries, particularly in Western Europe, as described in Chapter Five.

Racism no longer works that way in contemporary Australia. It does exist in several forms: first, racism towards Aborigines has been continuous and intense throughout Australian history. At present, anti-Aboriginal racism takes the form of prejudiced attitudes, and of economic and social marginalization. Second, some migrant groups are victims of structural racism, through mechanisms of labour market segmentation (as outlined in Chapter Two). Third, the Blainey Debate of 1984, as an attempt to develop an embracing racist ideology, did point to the existence of racist attitudes which could be articulated and mobilized.

Yet the fact that the Blainey Debate did not lead to a substantial and lasting racist mobilization points to the non-viability of racism as an ideology of the Australian nation today. Anti-Aboriginal racism persists because of the structural marginality of black Australians. An ideology based on anti-migrant racism is a non-starter just because migrants are structurally incorporated: as workers, small business owners, professionals and as citizens with civil and political rights. There is no significant social grouping which has a material interest in their dis-integration. And even if there were, there is no conceivable mechanism to achieve this. Blainey and Ruxton were aware enough of this not to direct their campaign against immigrants in general, but against Asians (and, later, Africans). The difference of skin-colour seemed to offer a chance for exclusionary policies (as the example of Britain indicated). It did indeed prove possible to mobilize anti-Asian feeling, but only on the streets and in the pubs. There was no significant political force or interest group willing to take it up for their own ends; it corresponded with nobody's interests.

The material reason for the non-viability of anti-migrant racism in Australia is the sheer size of their contribution to society and the economy, together with their incorporation into the people as voting citizens. The ideological reason is the existence of the doctrine of multiculturalism, as a reasonably successful way of managing the potential conflicts of a multi-ethnic society. Multiculturalism does bear racist elements: the recourse to primordiality as a basis for ethnic identity; the acceptance of ethnic chauvinisms (and sexism) as acceptable elements of cultures. The neo-conservative project of multiculturalism (of the Fraser-Zubrzycki-Galbally type) trades on such regressive elements as aspects of a divide-and-rule strategy for social control in a multi-ethnic society. The social democratic variant of multiculturalism is open to this critique too, despite its generalist social policy aims, for it cannot manage without recourse to culturalism in the final analysis. Multiculturalism is based on a construction of community through a celebration and fossilization of differences, which are then subsumed into an imagined community of national cohesion. It is a necessary project for the contemporary Australian-state, and one which makes an overt return to a racist definition of the nation impossible.

But that does not necessarily mean that the multicultural project can succeed. We argue that it is too contradictory and limited an ideology to gain wide and enduring support. To start with, multicul-turalism is not an accurate statement of power relations in Australia, where there is still a clear link between ethnicity (or more accurately, migrant worker status) and socio-economic life chances. Second, multiculturalism postulates at best an equal chance to be unequal, in a society where inequality is growing and welfare declining. It fails to address the fundamental dimensions of inequality: the ways in which ethnicity overlays class and gender. Third, cultural pluralism can actually preserve and deepen inequality, by creating separate and in-ferior educational and social systems for different groups. Fourthly, multiculturalism, despite the declarations on its relevance to all Aus-tralians, is not an ideology that has much attraction for the Anglo majority. The constant changes and re-evaluations of multicultural policies indicates how contradictory and ephemeral the ideology is.

The answer to this dilemma is not to abandon multiculturalism, but to concentrate our efforts on combatting the structural factors which maintain inequality. In the context of a struggle against economic and social marginalization, it will be possible to resolve the issue of ethnic separatism: all individuals and communities should have the right to cultural autonomy in a society based on equal social, economic and political rights for everyone irrespective of gender, race, ethnicity or class background. This implies combat-ting racist and sexist attitudes and institutions, both in Australian society, and in all of its subcultures. Our society will continue to be made up of communities of varying character, but such variation mut cease to be a focus for discrimination or disadvantage.

Options for Australia

What possibilities are available to Australia as we enter the third century of white settlement? We see four options:

1) Inequality plus imagined community

This means the continued integration of the economy as part of the world market, but with the development of a firm ideological basis for national identity, leading to a strong commitment to the Aus-tralian nation-state. This option, as spelt out by the New Right, seems highly unlikely to succeed, given the problems of Australian national identity described in this book. Attempts to create a general 'we-feeling' through sport, life-style symbols or indeed through the Bicentenary, have had no enduring success.

2) Inequality plus state repression

This is the 'Latin American' model, in which social and political divi-sions become too sharp to be accommodated in concensus-type parliamentary politics. If the Australian economy really moves into the 'Banana Republic' mode envisaged by Keating in 1986, and no equitable way of sharing the burden can be found, so that the billion-aires get richer and the number of people in poverty grows, then a peaceful solution may not be possible. Under similar pressures, formally democratic states in Latin America (Chile, Uruguay) succumbed to military dictatorships in the 1970s. This option seems possible, but not likely, for concensus politics have certainly not broken down here yet.

3) Inequality plus fragmentation and quiescence

In this option the breakdown of social solidarity takes the form not of polarization, but of fragmentation. Politics becomes increasingly meaningless, as the lack of real power of parliaments can no longer be concealed. Since the decisions are made in the stock exchanges of Tokyo, London and New York, and in the international corporate bureaucracies, why bother anyway? The result is hopelessness, hedonism and retreat into the private sphere. Protest takes the form of life-styles and sub-cultural pressure groups, and can easily be co-opted by the leisure industries. Increasing drug and alcohol addiction, fundamentalist religion, mental illness and violence are products of the real powerlessness of the social being. Politics shift from interests to values, providing a focus for New Right ideologies of family, individuality and competition. This seems the most likely scenario of all, for it is simply an extrapolation of existing trends.

4) Equality plus real communality

An alternative to these less than inspiring possibilities is a society based on the best elements of national Australian tradition, the most important postulates of multiculturalism, and the needs and interests of the broad majority of the population. Such a political and cultural reorientation would transcend any idea of nationalism, nation-state or simply imagined community.

The Australian traditions which should be reasserted are not those of colonization or war, but those of the 'fair go', that is, of social justice for all. The image of Australia which should be brought back is that of the 'workingman's paradise', though the racist and sexist aspects of this ideal would need to be worked through and modified.

The aspects of multiculturalism worth maintaining are the principles of cultural self-determination and of cosmopolitan identity. They must be linked to measures to meet the specific needs of discriminated and disadvantaged groups, and include policies to overcome structural marginalization and labour market segmentation, and to combat racism and prejudice.

Above all, the history of white racism and genocide against the Aborigines must become a central theme of education and public debate, and an accommodation with the Aborigines must be achieved through payment of reparations and Land Rights legislation. Steps must be taken to improve dramatically the economic and social situation of the Aboriginal population, not through welfare measures, but through making adequate resources available to Aboriginal communities and these being placed under their own control.

Any such strategy must be based on an attempt to redefine the basis of social organization, and to move away from a political emphasis on the nation-state. Australian life today is determined as much by events on the local level, as by those on the level of world politics and economics. In Britain, it has been local politics which have provided hope in the wasteland of Thatcherism. There is no contradiction between attempts to build community and bring about change at the local level, political work in the national arena, and participation in world politics.

The Bicentenary could have been an occasion for celebration. The opportunity was thrown away by Australian political leaders' unwillingness to face up to the real issues and problems. Once the decision was taken to ignore Aboriginal demands for real expiation, the Bicentenary became a lost cause. It changed from something with potential social meaning to a public relations exercise. Bicentennial Authority propaganda let the cat out of the bag, by calling for the inclusion of youth, women, ethnic groups, Aborigines and the handicapped in the celebrations. The conclusion was inescapable: only white Anglo middle-class men really had anything to celebrate in Australia; the inclusion of the rest was tokenism. If the Bicentenary had been concerned with helping to create an all-embracing society, it would have been based on real changes, designed not only to secure equality for the groups mentioned, but also to bring in others, whose marginalization makes them invisible for those in power: the unemployed, those living below the poverty line, the industrial casualties, the financially, culturally and socially deprived.

The Bicentenary is yet another indication of how the concept of the nation has become ideological and exclusionary, failing to embrace most of the population. The group which wields power and benefits from it gets ever smaller. More and more of us are members of minorities. Building communality means taking the real situation in our cities, suburbs and country areas as a starting point, adopting political and economic forms which correspond with the needs and interests of the many groups who are voiceless at present, and working for change everywhere. We do not need a new ideology of nationhood. We need to transcend the nation, as an increasingly obsolete relic of early industrialism. Our aim must be community without nation.

Bibliography

ALFA: *Major Findings and Recommendations*, Melbourne: Monash University 1987.

Benedict Anderson, *Imagined Communities*, London: Verso 1983.

Alan Ashbolt, 'Godzone: myth and reality', *Meanjin*, Vol.25, No.4, December 1966.

Allen Attwood, 'Our elusive soul', *Time Australia*, 21 July 1986.

Australian Bureau of Statistics, *The Labour Force*, Catalogue No.63100.

Australian Council on Population and Ethnic Affairs, *Multiculturalism for All Australians: Our Developing Nationhood*, Canberra, 1977.

Australian Institute of Multicultural Affairs (AIMA), *Reducing the Risk; Unemployment Migrant Youth and Labour Market Programs*, Melbourne: AIMA 1985.

M. Barker, *The New Racism*, London: Junction Books, 1981.

David Barnett, 'Dividing Australia: how Government money for ethnics is changing our nation,' *The Bulletin*, 18 February 1986.

R. Birrell and A. Seitz, *The Ethnic Problem in Education: The Emergence and Definition of an Issue*, Paper for AIMA Conference, Melbourne 1986.

Geoffrey Blainey, *All for Australia*, Sydney: Methuen Haynes, 1984.

Geoffrey Blainey, 'The Asianization of Australia', Melbourne *Age*, 20 March 1984.

B. Bullivant, 'Are Anglo-Australian students becoming the new self-deprived in comparison with ethnics?', Melbourne: Monash University 1986.

I. Burnley, 'Convergence or occupational and residential segmentation?' in: *Australian and New Zealand Journal of Sociology*, No.1.

S. Castles, 'The guests who stayed — the debate on 'Foreigners Policy' in the German Federal Republic', *International Migration Review*, Vol.19 No.71 Fall 1985.

S. Castles 'The European guestworker — an obituary', in: *International Migration Review*, Vol.20, No.76, Winter 1986.

S. Castles, 'Migrants and minorities in post-Keynesian capitalism: the West German case', in: M. Cross, (ed.), *Racial Minorities and Industrial Change*, Cambridge University Press 1987.

S. Castles, *Here for Good — Western Europe's New Ethnic Minorities* (with the assistance of Heather Booth and Tina Wallace), London: Pluto Press 1984.

S. Castles, 'The function of labour migration in Western European capitalism' (with Godula Kosack), *New Left Review* No.73, 1972.

S. Castles and G. Kosack, *Immigrant Workers and Class Structure in Western Europe*, London: Oxford University Press 1973 and 1985.

S. Castles and others, *Patterns of Disadvantage among the Overseas Born and their Children*, Wollongong: Centre for Multicultural Studies 1986.

Centre for Contemporary Cultural Studies, *The Empire Strikes Back*, London: Hutchinson, 1982.

B. Chifley, 'Australia's immigration policy', *Current Notes* 20:5 April 1949.

Lauchlan Chipman, 'The menace of multiculturalism', *Quadrant*, April 1986.

L. J. M. Cooray, 'Multiculturalism in Australia: who needs it?', *Quadrant*, April 1986.

J. Collins, 'The political economy of post-war migration' in: E. L. Wheelwright and K. Buckley (eds), *Essay in the Political Economy of Australian Captialism*, Vol.1, Sydney: ANZ Book Company 1975.

J. Collins, 'Immigration and class: the Australian experience', in G. Bottomley and M. de Lepervanche (eds), *Ethnicity, Class and Gender in Australia*, Sydney: George Allen & Unwin 1984.

Commonwealth Immigration Advisory Council Report, Canberra 1946.

H. E. Coombs, *Trial Balance*, Melbourne: Macmillan 1981.

Bill Cope, *Racism and Naturalness*, paper for the Cultural Construction of Race Conference, University of Sydney, 4-5 August 1985, Social Literacy Monograph Series, Sydney.

Bill Cope and Michael Morrissey, *The Blainey Debate and the Critics of Multiculturalism*, paper for the Australian Institute for Multicultural Affairs National Research Conference, 14-16 May 1986.

L. F. Crips, *Ben Chifley: an Autobiography*, London: Longmans 1961.

Marie de Lepervanche, 'Australian Immigrants 1788-1940', in: E. L. Wheelwright and K. Buckley (eds), *Essays in the Political Economy of Australian Capitalism*, Vol.1, Sydney: ANZ Book Company 1975.

Department of Immigration and Ethnic Affairs, *Don't Settle for Less — Report of the Committee for Stage 1 of the Review of Migrant and Multicultural Programs and Services*, Canberra: AGPS 1986.

K. Dohse *Ausländische Arbeiter und Bürgerliche Staat*, Konigstein: Hain 1981.

F. Engels, 'The English elections', in: Marx and Engels, *On Britain*, Moscow: Foreign Languages Publishing House 1962.

J. Esser and J. Hirsch, 'Ein poliitsches Regulierungsmodell fur den 'nachfordistischen' Kapitalismus', in *Prokla*, No.56, September 1984.

A. Faulkner and D. Storer, 'The Georgiou report', *Migration Action*, Vol.1, 1982.

E. K. Fisk, *The Aboriginal Economy in Town and Country*, Sydney: George Allen & Unwin 1985.

Brian Fitzpatrick, *The Australian People, 1788-1945*, Melbourne University Press 1951.

F. Froebel, J. Heinrichs and O. Kreye, *The New International Division of Labour*, Cambridge University Press 1980.

Galbally Report on Migrant Services and Programs, Canberra: AGPS 1978.

E. Gellner, *Nations and Nationalism*, Oxford: Basil Blackwell 1983.

R. Gollan, *Radical and Working Class Politics*, Melbourne University Press 1960.

A. Grassby, *A Multi-Cultural Society for the Future*, Immigration Reference Paper, Australia, Department of Immigration, Canberra: AGPS 1973.

M. Hartwig, 'Capitalism and Aborigines', in: E. L. Wheelwright and K. Buckley (eds), *Essays in the Political Economy of Australian Capitalism*, Vol.3, Sydney: ANZ Book Company 1978.

D. Horne, *The Public Culture*, London and Sydney: Pluto Press 1986.

G. Hugo, *Changing Distribution and Age Structure of Birthplace Groups in Australia 1976-81*, Adelaide: National Institute of Labour Studies 1983.

A. Jakubowicz, 'State and ethnicity: multiculturalism as ideology', in: J. Jupp (ed.), *Ethnic Politics in Australia*, Sydney: George Allen & Unwin 1984.

A. Jakubowicz, 'Ethnicity, multiculturalism and neo-conservatism', in G. Bottomley and M. de Lepervanche (eds), *Ethnicity, Class and Gender in Australia*, Sydney: George Allen & Unwin 1984.

Fredrick Jameson, 'Post-modernism, or the cultural logic of late capitalism', *New Left Review*, No.146, July-August 1984, pp.53-93.

J. Jupp, 'Australian immigration 1788-1873', in: F. Milne and P. Shergold (eds), *The Great Immigration Debate*, Sydney: FECCA 1984.

Mary Kalantizis, Bill Cope and Diana Slade, *The Language Question: The Maintenance of Languages other than English*, Canberra: AGPS 1986.

A. Kessler-Harris and V. Yans-McLaughlin, 'European immigrant groups', in: T. Sowell (ed.),*American Ethnic Groups*, New York: The Urban Institute 1978.

P. E. F. Kirby, *Report of the Committee of Inquiry into Labour Market Programs*, Canberra: AGPS 1985.

Frank Knopfelmacher, 'The case against multiculturalism', in R. Manne (ed.), *The New Conservatism in Australia*, Melbourne: Oxford University Press 1982.

R. Kriegler and J. Sloan, *Technological Change and Migrant Employment*, Adelaide: National Institute of Labour Studies 1984.

C. Lever-Tracy and M. Quinlan, *Breaking Down the Barriers: Asian Immigrants and Australian Trade Unions*, Brisbane: Griffith University no date.

J. Lyng, *Non-Britishers in Australia*, Melbourne University Press, 1935.

Humphrey McQueen, *A New Britannia*, Ringwood Victoria: Penguin 1970.

J. Martin, *The Migrant Presence*, Sydney: George Allen & Unwin 1978.

J. Martin and P. Meade, *The Educational Experience of Sydney High School Students Report No.1*, Canberra: AGPS 1979.

P. Meade, *The Educational Experience of Sydney High School Students Report No.1*, Canberra: AGPS 1979.

R. Miles, 'Labour migration, racism and capital accumulation in Western Europe', in: *Capital and Class*, 28 Spring 1986.

F. Milne and P. Shergold (eds), *The Great Immigration Debate*, Sydney: Federation of Ethnic Community Councils of Australia 1984.

N. Mistillis, *Destroying Myths: Second-Generation Australian's Educational Achievements*, Melbourne: Monash University 1986 (unpublished paper).

D. Moynihan, *The Negro Family: The Case for National Action*, Washington D. C.: Government Printing Office 1965.

Tom Nairn, *The Break-up of Britain*, London: Verso 1981.

OECD, *Continuous Reporting System on Migration (SOPEMI) 1985*, Paris: OECD 1986.

A. C. Palfreeman, 'The White Australian Policy', in: F. Stevens (ed.) *Racism the Australian Experience*, Brookvale: ANZ Book Company 1971.

A. Pinkney, *The Myth of Black Progress*, Cambridge University Press 1984.

Report of Commonwealth State and Territory Ethnic Affairs Officers on Migrant Unemployment, Melbourne: AIMA 1986.

C. D. Rowley, *Recovery*, Ringwood Victoria: Pengiun 1986.

S. Sassen-Koob, 'Capital mobility and labour migration: their expression in core cities', in: M. Cross (ed.), *Racial Minorities and Industrial Change*, Cambridge University Press 1987.

Lord Scarman, *The Scarman Report — The Brixton Disorders 10-12 April 1981*, Harmondsworth: Penguin 1982.

Hugh Seton-Watson, *Nations and States: An Enquiry into the Origins of Nations and the Politics of Nationalism*, London: Methuen 1977.

T. Sowell, *Markets and Minorities*, New York: Basic Books 1981.

W. E. H. Stanner, 'The Australian Way of Life', in: W. V. Aughterson (ed.) *Taking Stock*, Melbourne: Cheshire 1953.

D. Storer, *Migrant Workers in Victoria: Trends in Employment and Segmentation*, Working Paper No.5, Melbourne: Victorian Ethnic Affairs Commission 1985.

D. Storer, *Migrant Workers Unemployment in Victoria: Trends and Policy Directions 1985*, Melbourne: Victorian Ehtnic Affairs Commission 1985.

TNC Workers Research, *Anti-Union Employment Practices — Final Report*, Sydney: TNC 1985.

United Nations Economic and Social Council, *Concise Report on Monitoring of Population Trends*, New York: United Nations 1978.

US Bureau of the Census, *Statistical Abstract of the United States*, 1985. Washington D.C.: USGOP 1984.

N. Viviani, *The Long Journey: Vietnamese Migration and Settlement in Australia*, Melbourne University Press 1984.

Russel Ward, *Man Makes History: World History from the Earliest Times of the Renaissance*, Sydney: Shakespeare Head Press 1952.

Richard White, *Inventing Australia*, Sydney: George Allen & Unwin 1981.

K. Whitfield, *The Australian Labour Market*, Sydney: Harper & Row 1987.

D. Wood and G. Hugo, *Distribution and Age Structure of the Australian Born with Overseas Born Parents*, Canberra: DIEA 1984.

E. O. Wright and Singelmann, 'Proletarianization in the Changing American Class Structure', *American Journal of Sociology*, Vol.88 Supplement.

Nira Yuval-Davis, 'Ethnic/Racial Divisions and the Nation in Britain and Australia', *Capital and Class*, Vol.88/1986, p.92.